First World War
and Army of Occupation
War Diary
France, Belgium and Germany

38 DIVISION
Headquarters, Branches and Services
Royal Army Ordnance Corps
Deputy Assistant Director Ordnance Services
1 March 1915 - 30 April 1919

WO95/2544/2

The Naval & Military Press Ltd
www.nmarchive.com
Published in association with The National Archives

Published by

The Naval & Military Press Ltd

Unit 10 Ridgewood Industrial Park,

Uckfield, East Sussex,

TN22 5QE England

Tel: +44 (0) 1825 749494

www.naval-military-press.com

www.nmarchive.com

This diary has been reprinted in facsimile from the original. Any imperfections are inevitably reproduced and the quality may fall short of modern type and cartographic standards.

© **Crown Copyright**
Images reproduced by permission of The National Archives, London, England, 2015.

Contents

Document type	Place/Title	Date From	Date To
Heading	WO95/2544/2 Deputy Assistant Director Ordnance Services		
Heading	38th Division D.A. Dir. Ordnance Serv. Dec 1915-Apr 1919		
Heading	38th Div Vol I Nov & Decr 15 Dec 15 Apr 19		
War Diary	Folkestone	27/11/1915	27/11/1915
War Diary	Merville	28/11/1915	04/12/1915
War Diary	Roquetoire	05/12/1915	19/12/1915
War Diary	Merville	20/12/1915	31/12/1915
War Diary	Merville	26/12/1915	28/12/1915
Heading	D.A.D.O. 38th Div. Vol 2		
War Diary	Merville	01/01/1916	31/01/1916
War Diary	Merville	06/01/1916	23/01/1916
Heading	D.A.D.O.S. 8th Div. Vol.3		
War Diary	Locon	31/01/1916	29/02/1916
Heading	D A D O S 38 Div Vol 4		
War Diary	Locon	01/03/1915	31/03/1915
Heading	War Diary Of D.A.D.O.S. 38th Division For Month Of April		
War Diary	Locon	06/04/1916	26/04/1916
War Diary	La Gorgue	06/05/1916	09/06/1916
War Diary	La Gorgue	05/06/1916	05/06/1916
War Diary	St. Venant	12/06/1916	15/06/1916
War Diary	Roellecourt	16/06/1916	26/06/1916
War Diary	Le Melliard	27/06/1916	30/06/1916
War Diary	Rubempre	01/07/1916	01/07/1916
War Diary	Lealvillers	02/07/1916	02/07/1916
War Diary	Treux	03/07/1916	11/07/1916
War Diary	Pont Remy	12/06/1916	14/06/1916
War Diary	Couin	15/06/1916	20/06/1916
War Diary	Bus Les Artois	29/07/1916	30/07/1916
War Diary	Esquelbecq	31/07/1916	20/08/1916
War Diary	Esquelbecq	18/08/1916	22/08/1916
War Diary	Poperinghe	21/08/1916	14/12/1916
War Diary	Esquelbecq	15/12/1916	12/01/1917
War Diary	Poperinghe	15/01/1917	11/06/1917
War Diary	Dragon Camp	12/06/1917	29/06/1917
War Diary	Norrent Fontes	30/06/1917	30/06/1917
Miscellaneous	D A Dir Ordinance Service		
War Diary	Norrent Fontes	01/07/1917	17/07/1917
War Diary	Proven	18/07/1917	21/07/1917
War Diary	Dragon Camp	22/07/1917	30/07/1917
War Diary	Dragon Camp	23/07/1917	06/08/1917
War Diary	Proven	07/08/1917	19/08/1917
War Diary	Dragon Camp	20/08/1917	31/08/1917
War Diary	Dragon Camp (28/A.9.cent)	01/09/1917	12/09/1917
War Diary	Bac St Maur	13/09/1917	31/12/1917
War Diary	Toutencourt	01/05/1918	24/08/1918
War Diary	Hedauville	25/08/1918	28/08/1918
War Diary	La Boisselle	29/08/1918	04/09/1918

War Diary	Les Boeufs	05/09/1918	11/09/1918
War Diary	Rocquigny	12/09/1918	01/10/1918
War Diary	Nurlu	02/10/1918	06/10/1918
War Diary	Epehy	07/10/1918	09/10/1918
War Diary	Villers Outreaux	10/10/1918	12/10/1918
War Diary	Bertry	13/10/1918	25/10/1918
War Diary	Forest	26/10/1918	05/11/1918
War Diary	Englefontaine	06/11/1918	07/11/1918
War Diary	Locquignol	08/11/1918	12/11/1918
War Diary	Aulnoye	13/11/1918	30/11/1918
Miscellaneous	Headquarters 38 Div.	15/01/1919	15/01/1919
War Diary	Aulnoye	01/12/1918	30/12/1918
War Diary	Pont Noyelles	31/12/1918	01/03/1919
War Diary	Poulainville	03/03/1919	30/04/1919

WO/95/26442

Deputy Assistant Director
Ordnance Services

38TH DIVISION

D. A. DIR. ORDNANCE SERV.

DEC 1915 - APR 1919

S.A.S.O. 38th Div.
Vol: I

121/7795

Nov & Dec. 15

Dec 15
Apr 19

Army Form C. 2118

WAR DIARY
or
INTELLIGENCE SUMMARY
(Erase heading not required.)

D.A.D.S.
38th Welsh Division

Place	Date	Hour	Summary of Events and Information	Remarks and references to Appendices
Folkestone	27.11.15	—	Left Folkestone for Boulogne with Advance party of the 38th (Welsh) Division.	
Merville	28.11.15 to 4.12.15	—	Attached to 2nd Division Merville until arrival of Division	
Roquetoire	5.12.15 to 19.12.15	—	38th Division commenced to arrive - billeted in training area with Railhead at STEENBECQUE. Large quantities of stores arrived, mainly winter clothing. Great difficulty in rapidly transferring stores to Units owing to long distance from Railhead.	
Merville	20.12.15 to 31.12.15	—	Division moved to Reserve Area with Railhead at MERVILLE. Supply & Ordnance Stores to Units made without any difficulty, supplies being received and issued the same day.	
"	26.12.15		Temp. Lieut H.P. Palmer joined for duty.	
"	28.12.15		" " " " " left to join 2nd Division 28.12.15	
"	"		" " " L.A.S. Storer joined for duty.	

M Stevens (Captain)
A.D.S/38 D.S.

StAP. 38E St.i.
Vol: 2
Tu'le

Army Form C. 2118

WAR DIARY
or
INTELLIGENCE SUMMARY

D.A.D.S. 38th Division January 1916

(Erase heading not required.)

Instructions regarding War Diaries and Intelligence Summaries are contained in F.S. Regs., Part II. and the Staff Manual respectively. Title Pages will be prepared in manuscript.

Place	Date	Hour	Summary of Events and Information	Remarks and references to Appendices
Merville	1st to 31st Jan 1916	—	Ordnance Stores received during the month regularly and were issued promptly.	
	17.1.16		" " " Temporary Lieut L.A.S. Stoneleigh A.V.D. appointed to join 19th Division	
			" " " B. Clifford A.V.D. joined for duty.	
	25.1.16		Divisional Troops to forward areas with Ordnance Departments at LOCON.	

J. Bosworth Carter
D.A.D.O.S.
31-1-16

A.A.D.O.S. 38th Div:
Vol: 3

WAR DIARY
or
INTELLIGENCE SUMMARY

DADOS. 38. Division Army Form C. 2118

13/?

Place	Date	Hour	Summary of Events and Information	Remarks and references to Appendices
LOCON	3/7/16		Capt. W.H. Townsend A.O.D left for duty at CALAIS. Temporary Lieut. B. Clifford. A.O.D. assumed duties of Divl. Ordnance Officer.	
	10/7/16		Divisional Armourers shop opened at LOCON. Four armourer Sergeants withdrawn from Battalions for duties at the shop. The repairing of arms and bicycles started at once.	
	14/7/16		Base changed from Southern to Northern for majority of Ordnance Stores. Last truck left S. Base to-day.	
	15/7/16		First truck with Ordnance stores from N. Base arrived.	
	to 29/7/16		Stores received regularly & issued promptly.	

M C Mott Lieut. A O D
DADOS. 38th Divn.

DADDY'S 3
3RD DD
Vol 4

Army Form C. 2118

WAR DIARY
or
INTELLIGENCE SUMMARY
(Erase heading not required.)

D.A.D.O.S. 38th Division.

Instructions regarding War Diaries and Intelligence Summaries are contained in F. S. Regs., Part II. and the Staff Manual respectively. Title Pages will be prepared in manuscript.

Place	Date	Hour	Summary of Events and Information	Remarks and references to Appendices
LOCON	March 1		Issue of 1st 'P.H.' anti gas Helmet in exchange for 'P' to all units completed.	
	9		26 Lewis Guns received and issued to Battalions, bringing up the numbers now held by each Battalion to six.	
	20		14,350 'PH Helmets received. All infantry battalions were issued with the second helmet in exchange for 'P' pattern.	
	21	3pm	Lieut. F.J. SPRANGER. D.A.D.O.S. 41st Division arrived from ENGLAND being attached for three days.	
	23		5,650 'P.H.' Helmets received. Issue of 2nd 'P.H. Helmet - for exchange for 'P' being completed to all units of the Division.	
	"	10am	Lieut. F.J SPRANGER departed for ENGLAND.	
	31		Eight Vickers Machine Guns received & issued.	
	31		Four 1½ inch medium T. Mortars received from SAINT VENANT and issued to Artillery Hd Qrs for Z/38 T.M. Battery. Ordnance Stores were received regularly & issued promptly during the month.	

N.R. Clifford Lieut.
D.A.D.O.S. 38th Div.

1875 Wt. W593/826 1,300,000 4/15 J.B.C. & A. A.D.S.S./Forms/C. 2118.

War Diary
of
D.A.D.O.S
38th Division
for month of April

A. J. Sturton
Lt
Acting D.A.D.O.S

30/4/16

WAR DIARY
INTELLIGENCE SUMMARY

Army Form C. 2118

D.A.D.O.S. 38th Division

Place	Date	Hour	Summary of Events and Information	Remarks and references to Appendices
LOCON	6 April		Started the return of Winter clothing today. 4,000 Undercoats Fur sent down to Base.	
	9 "		Four 3" Stokes Mortars received, and issued to 113/2 T.M. Batty, 2, to 114/1 T.M. Batty, 2.	
	14th "		Temp: Lieutenant A.J. STURTON. A.O.D. joined for duty. Four 2" French Mortars received from Base, and issued to 2/38 Battery, to replace four 1½" T.M's.	
	15th "		Four 1½" Trench Mortars returned to Base.	
	16th "		Ordnance Refilling Point moved to LA GORGUE. (Divisional H.Q. moving into the new area on next day)	
	18th "		12,800 P.H. Helmets antigas received, being part of Divisional Reserve of P.H. Helmets completed to 20,000.	
	20th "		1,000 (Steel) Helmets French received	
	21st "		Sec. Capt. B. CLIFFORD left for 10 days leave on a Ten Scheme	
	25th "		A.J. STURTON took on the duties of D.A.D.O.S.	Manilin Capt A.D.O.S. 38 Div.
	" "		Four 2" T.M. Bos received from Base & sent to 6 X D Coy	
	26th "		Four 1½"-T.M. T's returned by X Btry & returned to Base	A.J. Sturton Lt for D.A.D.O.S. 38 Div

Army Form C. 2118

WAR DIARY D.A.D.O.S. 38th Division. Vol 6
or
INTELLIGENCE SUMMARY
(Erase heading not required.)

Place	Date	Hour	Summary of Events and Information	Remarks and references to Appendices
LA GORGUE	6 May 1916		Temp. Capt. B. CLIFFORD D.A.D.O.S. returned from leave of absence in ENGLAND.	
	7 "		Temp. Lieut. A.J. STURTON. A.O.D. left for duty with 39th Division.	
	8 "		One Lewis gun received, to replace one destroyed by shell fire — (14th R.W. Fusiliers.)	
	10 "		1000 Helmets, steel, received.	
	12 "		1000 do do do	
	16 "		1000 do do do	
	24 "		Reorganisation of D.A.C. & re-arrangement of R.F.A. Batteries complete.	
	26 "		Infantry Battalion now completed with Steel helmets to establishment.	
	27 "		Two 3" Stokes Mortars received & issued.	
	29 "		Four 3" " " "	
	30 "		Started re-painting of the steel helmets of the Division accordance with the pattern helmet received from Base.	
	31st "		Four 4" Light T.M.s and five 3.7" L.T.M.s handed over to O.O. XI Corps. Eight Vickers Guns returned to Base — surplus on arrival of Brigade Machine Gun Batteries.	
	1st–31st		Inspecting the transport vehicles (horse drawn) of the Division	

B. Clifford Capt.
D.A.D.O.S. 38 Div

WAR DIARY
INTELLIGENCE SUMMARY
(Erase heading not required.)

Army Form C. 2118

June 1916

D.A.D.O.S.
38th Division

Vol 7 Jun.

Place	Date	Hour	Summary of Events and Information	Remarks and references to Appendices
LA GORGUE	1st to 9th June		Inspecting Transport vehicles of the Division. Completed same in last named Unit. General state very poor after 6 months in France. 30% of the brakes of Lewis G.S. wagons were missing, having been taken off when the rods supporting the bar of brake are apparently too light a pattern & constantly broken. Received some 3" Stokes Mortars. D.D.O.S. First Army inspected stores etc.	
	5 "		Moved Ordnance Re-filling point to ST. VENANT, on Division moving South.	
ST. VENANT	12 "		Railhead changed to CHOCQUES	
	13 "			
	15 "		" TINQUES. Moved Ordnance re-filling point to	
ROELLECOURT	16 "		ROELLECOURT in the Third Army Area.	
	18 "		Visit from A.D.O.S. XVII Corps. D.D.O.S. Third Army.	
	21 "		Received 26 Lewis Guns & raised them to the Battalions, completing the number per Battalion in this Division to 8.	
	26 "		Divisional Headquarters moved to LE MELLIARD & Ordnance Re-filling point to the same place.	
LE MELLIARD	27 "		Railhead changed to FREVENT.	
	28 "		" " TIENVILLERS - CANDAS. Since 12 P. inst difficulty was experienced in clearing trucks owing to late arrival on several occasions at the same time, having been recognised on charge of Railhead.	
	30 "		Division moved to RUBEMPRE district with Ordnance re-filling point in that village. During all above moves stores were broken up at Railhead & taken to the supply refilling points for distribution. The reserve of 30,000 Box Respirators, Helmets, regarding 5 lorry loads caused hindrance to easy working of this system.	

B.G. Gifford Capt. DADOS 38 Div.

July

Army Form C. 2118

P.A.D.O.S.
38th Division
Vol 8

WAR DIARY
or
INTELLIGENCE SUMMARY
(Erase heading not required.)

1st Sheet.

Instructions regarding War Diaries and Intelligence Summaries are contained in F.S. Regs., Part II. and the Staff Manual respectively. Title Pages will be prepared in manuscript.

Place	Date 1916	Hour	Summary of Events and Information	Remarks and references to Appendices
RUBEMPRÉ	1 July	5.30pm	Received orders to prepare to move Eastward at 7pm. Ready to time & moved at 9pm. according to orders.	
MEALYVILLERS	2 "		Railhead changed to LEALVILLERS. Railhead at CANDAS.	
TREUX	3 "		Moved with Div. H.Q. to TREUX. Received 98 Lewis Gun handcarts. 4000 which were taken with us were left at LEALVILLERS during three 2 mins and were brought to TREUX in the 5th int.	
	5 "		Railhead changed to MERICOURT sur L'ANCRE. Divisional H.Q. moved to E GROVE TOWN. Ordnance Dump remaining at TREUX.	
	6 July		The Division relieved the 7th Division in the front line and two Brigades of Infantry went into action at MAMETZ WOOD. One Lewis Gun reported destroyed on 7th inst. Railhead changed to EDGE MILL. One Lewis Gun received & issued, another reported destroyed. Divisional care out of the line in evening of D.H.Q. returned to TREUX.	
	10			
	11			
PONT REMY	12		The Division less its Artillery and one Brigade of Infantry, moved to reserve area with H.Q. and Ordnance Dump at PONT REMY. As were thought, arranged with the relieving Division to exchange reserve of P.H. Helmets.	
	13		Railhead changed to LONGPRE. Visited all the Inf. Brigade H.Q. to ascertain important deficiencies in arms & equipment & found that many boxes of Lewis Guns & some machine Guns had not been reported, so called for demands from all units. As a result a further 18 Lewis & 3 Vickers Guns were demanded from Base. The following above not losses of those going during the actions of 6.7. — 11.7. inst:—	

Lewis Guns → 9   13   22   8   14
Vickers M.G.'s   3   nil   3   2   1
                 12   13   25 10   15

to replace Lost.total. Salved & repaired. Total losses

Army Form C. 2118

WAR DIARY
OR
INTELLIGENCE SUMMARY

(Erase heading not required.)

D.A.D.O.S. 38th Division

2nd Sheet

Instructions regarding War Diaries and Intelligence Summaries are contained in F.S. Regs., Part II. and the Staff Manual respectively. Title Pages will be prepared in manuscript.

Place	Date	Hour	Summary of Events and Information	Remarks and references to Appendices
PONT REMY	14 July		Orderly sent the lorries & equipment & stores proceeding. Found it difficult to visit the widely separated units, i.e. 2 Brigades in Main area, one at WARLOY, all the Artillery in MEAULTE area and the Salvage Dumps on the CARNOY-FRICOURT road. During this period, from 11th onwards, lorries with Ordnance Stores were sent out to pre-arranged points where they were issued to the troops as often as possible & issues made. It was not possible to do this daily to all of them.	
COVIN	15 "		Moved to BEAUVAL at 9 a.m. Shortly after arrival received orders that Div. H.Q. and to go on to COVIN, so moved on again & found that the Ordnance of the Division we were relieving were not moving out till next day.	
	17 "		Railhead changed to BELLE EGLISE. With stores and some large receipts from Base (the re-equipping of the Division was carried on and was practically complete by the 20th not Salvage Coy (from the late Divisional fighting area) arrived with three lorry loads of salvaged stores.) to which date the last of the machine guns was received from Base.	
BUS les ARTOIS	20 "			
	29 "		Moved with Div. H.Q. to BUS les ARTOIS, then to reserve of whole Division.	
	30 "		Northward to 2nd Army reserve area. Moved to LILLERS for the night and on to ESQUELBECQ next morning. The units of the Division going by train on these two days. Exchanged P.H. Helmets with outgoing Divn.	
ESQUELBECQ	31 "		Railhead changed to ARNEKE. During the month Ordnance trains arrived somewhat irregularly and were seldom sent on the supply train, causing a hindrance to regular issuing to units & useless journeys of the lorries & staff to Railhead.	

B. Williams Capt.
D.a.D.O.S. 38 Div.

1875 Wt. W593/826 1,000,000 4/15 J.B.C. & A. A.D.S.S./Forms/C. 2118.

WAR DIARY DADOS. 38th Division

INTELLIGENCE SUMMARY

Vol 4

Army Form C. 2118

(Erase heading not required.)

Place	Date 1916	Hour	Summary of Events and Information	Remarks and references to Appendices
ESQUELBECQ	1 Aug		20 trucks arrived at new railhead (ARNEKE) 10 km.	
	5"		Received 15,000 P.H.G. Helmets antigas. This completed the issue of 1 per Officer & man for the whole Division. Received also 1,000 Steel Helmets.	
	6th to 20th		All the Vickers Guns of the Machine Gun Companies were brought in to the Divisional Armourers' Shop for general overhaul & repair, while the Division was in the Reserve Area.	
	18		1,000 Steel Helmets received	
	21st & 22nd		2,500 Magazines Lewis Gun received. All demands for replacements done to losses when in the Somme, actively now satisfied.	
POPERINGHE	21.		Moved to POPERINGHE (A.4. b.8.2. Sheet 27) when Division moved into the line with Div H.Q. at ST. SIXTE. Reserve of P.H. Helmets brought in. Railhead changed to POPERINGHE. Reverted to anytime by which all units called daily at Ordnance Dump for stores, & all returned & unserviceable stores received there for transmission to Rail-head.	
	23			
	29.		Started small Divisional Boot-repairing shop for Div H.Q. & other small units without means of doing their own repairs.	

31/8/16.

BCliffard Capt.
DADOS. 38 Div.

WAR DIARY
or
INTELLIGENCE SUMMARY

Army Form C. 2118

D.A.D.O.S. 38th Division

38/ September 1916 Vol 6

Place	Date	Hour	Summary of Events and Information	Remarks and references to Appendices
POPERINGHE	Sept 2		52 Hyposcopes for Lewis Guns received, completing the establishment of 1 per 2 guns for the Division.	
	4		71 (Revolver) Pistols Webley received for arming 50% of personnel of Medium Trench Mortar Batteries. Also 1200 Helmets T.P.	
	5		Issue of "First" blankets to units started today on receipt of a truck load. Received also the first consignment of small box respirators from Base.	
	8		Issued small type respirators to one Infantry Brigade, no other units having yet been trained in their use.	
	10		Moved the Ordnance Dump with Office, ammunition shop & bootmakers premises at A.2.a.2.5 sheet 28. Completed issue of 12th Blanket.	
	17		Received the Divisional reserve of socks viz 5000 pairs. It is a more convenient reserve of socks in latter part of month due to more very wet weather & making it all units to full establishment. Which to time on 25th for 3,000 to you make up reserve. Reported a	
	21		Railhead changed to PROVEN.	
	25		Very heavy demands on socks in latter part of month due to more very wet weather & making it all units to full establishment. Which to time on 25th for 3,000 to you make up reserve. Reported a serious shortage of Borlers for Kitchens travelling, very few having been received from base for past two months	

Montford Capt
D.A.D.O.S 38 Div

30/9/16.

Army Form C. 2118

38

D.A.D.O.S.
38th Division

October 1916.
Vol 11

WAR DIARY
INTELLIGENCE SUMMARY
(Erase heading not required.)

Instructions regarding War Diaries and Intelligence Summaries are contained in F. S. Regs., Part II. and the Staff Manual respectively. Title Pages will be prepared in manuscript.

Place	Date	Hour	Summary of Events and Information	Remarks and references to Appendices
POPERINGHE	Oct 1st to 3/10		Ordnance Stores have received regularly & promptly issued to units throughout the month. Large quantities of winter clothing, blankets and Gum Boots being handled & disposed of without difficulty.	
	13		Received Splinter Goggles for whole Division	
	20		A good supply of Boilers, Kitchen, Travelling. Over 100 of these had been outstanding for some months.	
	21		Received 28 Haversacks Lewis Gun, completing all Battalions to 1 per gun, & 10 & per Battalion.	
	22		Received first consignment of Blankets for issue if the weather for men.	
	23		D.D.O.S. Second Army inspected the Mess & stores.	
	23		1000 things have received issued. Thirty can be fastened, then only if the cold weather. Considerable quantities of Machine Gun & Lewis Gun parts were received during the month & which have since hitherto been large expenses in the Division.	
	31		All issues of winter clothing have been completed except 3000 Blankets 5000 Jerkins Leather & 9000 drawers woolen	

M.W.Wm Capt
D.A.D.O.S. 38 Div.

Army Form C. 2118

D.A.D.O.S. 38th Division
November 1916
Vol 12

WAR DIARY
or
INTELLIGENCE SUMMARY
(Erase heading not required.)

Place	Date	Hour	Summary of Events and Information	Remarks and references to Appendices
POPERINGHE	2nd		9,000 drawers woollen received and issued. The winter scale of these includes 1 pr mounted men is not popular in this Division & two drawers of cotton drawn in preference to the 1 pair woollen. + 1 pair cotton as laid down in G.R.O. 1824.	
	8		3,000 Milanets received	
	9		5,000 Wading coats prs received. All issues of winter clothing now completed	
	12		Completed issue of 1 pair shorts P.S. to scale of 1 pair per mounted man	
	14		Two 4.5 Howitzers (guns only) received to replace two with cracked jackets. These were taken up by lorry at night to the gun positions & the defective guns brought back & returned to Base on 15th.	
	15			
	18		Supply railhead changed to "DESELHOEK", that for Ordnance to POPERINGHE.	
	26		Received 12 Lewis guns and issued them to Battalions, completing them to 10 per Batt'n, except the Pioneers who hold 8 only. During the month all the Lewis Guns & Vickers of this Div't Brigades were examined & overhauled in D.A.D.O.S. Armourers Shop & the spare parts checked through & deficiencies demanded from Base.	

30/11/16

MCClifford Capt.
D.A.D.O.S. 38th Div.

Army Form C. 2118

D.A.D.D.S. No/5
38 Division
Dec. 1916

WAR DIARY
INTELLIGENCE SUMMARY
(Erase heading not required.)

Place	Date	Hour	Summary of Events and Information	Remarks and references to Appendices
POPERINGHE	Dec 3		Received orders for one Lewis Gun & one Vickers Gun destroyed by enemy in recent bombardment of our trenches.	
	6		These two guns now received & issued. Telephoned to Base for two.	
	14		Moved with Divisional H.Q. to ESQUELBECQ in Reserve area.	
ESQUELBECQ	15		Railhead changed to PROVEN. Found it necessary to change method of distributing stores owing to the widely separated units being no longer able to call at a central dump. Stores are now split up at Rail-head into the four lorries — one for each Brigade Group & moved the same day as the "supply" refilling points. No trucks arrived today.	
	22		16 lorry have been detached from the supply train & Needless journey to Railhead.	
	23		Two days stores at Railhead today. He 4 lorries were in consequent to take them all up to refilling points so some were dumped & issued next day.	
	24		Wired to Base for two Lewis Guns to replace two lost to the enemy in this recent raid of our trenches.	
	27		Two Lewis Guns received & issued.	
	31		Two trucks due today, only one — with a water cart on it - arrived, the other apparently was not sent off from Base.	

N.R. Williams Capt
D.A.D.D.S. 38 Div

31/12/16

Army Form C. 2118

Vol /

WAR DIARY
~~OR~~
INTELLIGENCE SUMMARY
(Erase heading not required.)

DADDS
38th Division
January 1917.

Instructions regarding War Diaries and Intelligence Summaries are contained in F. S. Regs., Part II. and the Staff Manual respectively. Title Pages will be prepared in manuscript.

Place	Date 1917 January	Hour	Summary of Events and Information	Remarks and references to Appendices
ESQUELBECQ	2		Twenty five Lewis Guns received, completing 11 battalions to 12 guns each. Two trucks with Box Respirators arrived. This was the first consignment for carrying out the exchange of all these issued prior to 21/9/16 in accordance with recent order.	
	3.		First day of bulk issues under the new scheme. The truck was parked & lorries only just able to take the whole contents.	
	5		Truck of Box Respirators arrived which was due yesterday. Also a truck of other stores. Lorries unable to take the whole and some was dumped at D.H.	
	6.		Supply train did not arrive today. Ltd. mon. additional lorry was obtained to clear cargo stores & there dumped yesterday.	
	7.		Two lorries advised as having arrived. The other came in 8/12.	
	10.		Heavy consignments again & difficulties - to clear units & lorries.	
	12		Truck advised but did not arrive.	
			Div H.Q. moved to ST. SIXTE. Ordnance Dump to POPERINGHE (Q.2.a.3.5, Sheet 28.)	
POPERINGHE	15.		Railhead changed to PESELHOEK Ad. Ordnance Trucks cut off at POPERINGHE.	
	19.		One Lewis Gun received in replacement of one destroyed by shell fire.	
	22		One Stokes Mortar (3") received in —	
	28.		Wired to Base for one 18 pdr gun to replace one worn out.	
	30		Received two Lewis Guns, completing all battalions to 12 guns except Pioneers. Wired to Base for one 4.5 How'r & carriage to replace one that —	
			Stores were received regularly during the month & issued same day at the Ration dumps. Pr.(?) difficulty was caused latterly through lateness of trains & sometimes with the very heavy consignments due to the new bulk arrangements.	

V.C. Clifton Capt.
DADDS 38 Div.

Army Form C. 2118.

WAR DIARY
or
INTELLIGENCE SUMMARY
(Erase heading not required.)

D.A.D.O.S.
38th Division
Feby. 1917

Vol/5

Instructions regarding War Diaries and Intelligence Summaries are contained in F.S. Regs., Part II and the Staff Manual respectively. Title pages will be prepared in manuscript.

Place	Date	Hour	Summary of Events and Information	Remarks and references to Appendices
POPERINGHE	Feby 2nd		Received from Base 24 Lewis Guns and nearest item completing numbers to 144 per Battn. except Pioneers. Received also one 18 Pdr. G.S. demanded on 28th Jany. Supply train very late. Unable to issue whole of stores same day.	
	4th		Purchased 780 metres of calico for blast sheets for artillery.	
	8th		Demanded two 18 Pdrs to replace two damaged by shell fire –	
	10th		" " " " "	
	12th		one 18 Pdr and carriage to replace one damaged by shell fire.	
	14th		Started inspection of Travelling Kitchens in accordance with Corps orders. Rain lightly shelled 2-4pm. Harboard the two 18 Pdrs demanded on 8th there not being reported on despatched from Base.	
	14th		Unable to use lorries for clearing Railhead, owing to their restriction. Obtained 8 wagons G.S. for the purpose. Rainy, two journeys each. The first loads taken to ration dump & issued.	
	15th		Two 18 Pdrs. Received clothing required to D.O.Hs for filling in the carriages	
	19th		C1286 Sept DONALD, A, A.O.C. arrived for duty – instruction in duties of Brigade W.O.	
	21st		One 4.5 How. Received, also one 18 Pdr. Batt issued to Batteries against them.	
	23rd		One 15 Pdr. Received and one also on the 24th. These were in replacement of others now out.	
	24th		Inspecting Travelling Kitchens ; opinion on 25th, D.D.O.S. Second Army inspected premises.	
	27th		Hour restrictions taken off. Used horsed transport for last time today. Stores were	

Army Form C. 2118.

D.A.D.O.S. 38 Bri.
Feby. 1917. contd.

WAR DIARY
or
INTELLIGENCE SUMMARY.
(Erase heading not required.)

Place	Date	Hour	Summary of Events and Information	Remarks and references to Appendices
POPERINGHE	Feby 27		usually cleared from Maillard in time for leaving at the station for filling parade but sometimes it required double journeys, not more than 10 vehicles being available on any one day.	
	28		The town was slightly shelled, and under orders from Town Major the staff and attached men were temporarily evacuated. One W&O & one man left on guard. During the month a large number of vehicles were condemned for wear, ten and eleven transport vehicles being demanded in replacement. One Vickers MGun, three 3" Stokes Mortars, and two Lewis guns were replaced. The Lewis guns being 'lost in action', & the others damaged by enemy fire. The supply of leather boots for boot repairs has been very short and for the last 18 days the Divisional Cops and Battalion Shops have been carrying out repairs with the best parts of unserviceable boots.	

W Buffon Capt
D.A.D.O.S. 38 Bri.

Army Form C. 2118.

D.A.D.O.S.
38. Division.
March. 1917

Vol 16

WAR DIARY
or
INTELLIGENCE SUMMARY.
(Erase heading not required.)

Place	Date	Hour	Summary of Events and Information	Remarks and references to Appendices
POPERINGHE	March 2		Inspecting Kitchens, Travelling, of 115 Brigade, and Vickers Belts.	
	4		Received 2 Lewis Guns indented for on 2nd inst in replacement of 2 captured from 14 R.W.F.; also one Vickers Gun for 113 M.G.Coy to replace one destroyed by enemy.	
			Ordnance Artificers were instructed to day by Divisional Commander and the O.C. d.G.R.S.	
	7		Received one 2" Trench Mortar in replacement of one condemned for wear.	
	9		Inspected the Travelling Kitchens of 16th Welsh Regt.	
	10		Two thirds of Leather demanded received to-day, and all Divisional Boot shops now able to carry out repairs properly, after doing them for over 2 weeks with old material.	
	11		Received 18 Pdr Q.T. for B/121. This gun has been on demand since 3rd inst.	
	12		Completed the Inspection of all the Travelling Kitchens in the Division, and sent in the lists of deficiencies in equipment in accordance with orders of Corps Commander.	
	14		Received 18 Pdr Q.F. & carriage for B/119. in replacement of one destroyed by "grenative". This gun had been on demand since 7th inst.	
	19		The town was lightly shelled to-day.	
	21		113 Infantry Brigade moved to Corps Reserve Area. BOLLEZEELE. Ordnance Stores will be issued to them as usual at the ration re-filling point on day of receipt from Base. Started to overhaul in the Boot Shop the whole of Lewis & Vickers Guns of this Brigade.	

Army Form C. 2118.

WAR DIARY
INTELLIGENCE SUMMARY.
(Erase heading not required.)

Instructions regarding War Diaries and Intelligence Summaries are contained in F.S. Regs. Part II. and the Staff Manual respectively. Title pages will be prepared in manuscript.

D.A.D.O.S.
38 Division.

March 1917 – (Cont)

Place	Date	Hour	Summary of Events and Information	Remarks and references to Appendices
POPERINGHE	March 22		The town was lightly shelled again. Most of the shells fell on the S. side & away from these premises.	
	25		24 Lewis Guns received today & issued 2 to each batt. All battalions now have 16 guns each, except the Pioneers who have 8 only. Received also one 18 Pdr Q.F. gun C/122 to replace one damaged by enemy fire. This gun was demanded on 16th inst.	
	28		176 Machine Gun Coy. joined the Division today, from England. 4 M.G. Coys are now in the Divn.	
	29		Visited the new M.G. Coy. Issued 130 Respirators and some other urgently required stores to them, and received indents for other items including 135 revolvers in replacement of the rifles with which they are armed.	
	30–31		114 Inf. Brigade exchanged places with 113 Brigade in Reserve area.	
	31		Received all the Lewis Guns of one Battalion of 114 Brigade for overhaul in Div. Shops. Stores were received regularly during the month & issued on day of receipt. There was a severe shortage of horse clippers & parts of clipping machines in early part of month, but all demands have now been met. The prevalence of mange greatly accentuated the need for these stores.	

N.C. Millar Capt
D.A.D.O.S. 38 Divn.
31/3/1917

Army Form C. 2118.

WAR DIARY
INTELLIGENCE SUMMARY
(Erase heading not required.)

D.A.D.O.S
38th Division
April 1917

Place	Date	Hour	Summary of Events and Information	Remarks and references to Appendices.
POPERINGHE	1		Visited Battalion Armourer & Boot repair shops at Zompit Lines & 114 Brigade.	
	2		All the Lewis Guns of 114 Welsh Regt overhauled in Divisional Armourershop.	
	4		Owing to the continued cold weather the order to commence the return of winter clothing today is cancelled	
	6		Indented for one 2" Trench Mortar to replace one damaged by shell fire.	
	13		Received above Mortar 10th, seven days after demand.	
	18		Entraining pieces for 120x Respirators received today from whole Division. Under instructions from General Staff priority of issue was given to the artillery.	
	21.		No soap was received with the bulk stores. One 4.5 Howitzer demanded to replace one with enlarged bore.	
	25		No soap or soda received today. Sent a lorry to DUNKIRK to purchase supplies of both for the Divisional Laundry & units.	
	27		Started taking in Winter Clothing from units for Respirators to Base. 1500 Horse Respirators received today. Amn (Ammunition) maintenance is to be established. 34 Pistols also received for issue to Officers. Nearly 500 rifles still due.	
	30.		Owing the months the Lewis & Vickers Guns of 113 Brigade and the remainder of the Lewis & Vickers guns of the 114 Brigade were overhauled in the Divl Armourers shop.	

J.B.Clifford Capt.
D.A.D.O.S. 38 Div.

Army Form C. 2118.

WAR DIARY
INTELLIGENCE SUMMARY
(Erase heading not required.)

D.A.D.O.S. 38th Division.

May 1917

Vol 18

Place	Date	Hour	Summary of Events and Information	Remarks and references to Appendices
POPERINGHE	May 1		Visited 115 Brigade H.Q. and 115 M.G. Coy & arranged for overhaul of Machine guns while unit is in reserve area.	
	2		Attended conference at Office of A.D.D.S. VIII Corps. Demanded one 4.5" Howitzer to replace one with enlarged bore. A few shells fell in the town this afternoon.	
	3		Fixed engagement of winter clothing – 4 trucks – sent to Base. Visited D.D.O.S. Second Army, 113 Brigade H.Q. & 113/122 R.F.A.	
	4		Visited D.C. Divl Train and 176 M.G. Coy.	
	6		One 2" T.M. demanded to replace one destroyed by Shell fire. Visited 16 R.W.F.	
	7		Visited major lines of Co of 113 Batteries, 119 Bde & 30 m VIII Corps. Sent off 2 trucks of Winter Clothing	
	8		" Corps & Divl Salvage Dumps, also 10 F Welsh Transport Lines.	
	9		" 114 Bgde H.Q. 113 Bgde H.Q. & 13 R.W.F. Two full trucks of stores received today from Base.	
	11		Two trucks of stores received, including 2 & 3" Stokes Mortars for 113 T.M.B. Visited D/119 & C/122. Sent off 3 trucks of Winter Clothing.	
	12		Visited 115 Bgde H.R. 10 SWB & 2 See DAC in Reserve area – BOLLEZEELE.	
	13		Received one 2" mortar. Visited 151 Field Coy R.E. & 15 R.W.F.	
	14		Went to HAZEBROUCK with D.A.Q.M.G. to Second Army Ordnance & R.E. Workshops.	
	15		Visited C/119 & 114 Bgde HQ. Three trucks of winter clothing and X Base.	
	17		Visited B/121. Reference horses in recent shelling from position.	
	18		Received one 18 Pdr, also large quantity of shorts for issue in exchange for F.S. bags being re-called.	
	20		Visited 12 S/W.B. & Transport Lines of 114 Inf Brigade.	

Army Form C. 2118.

WAR DIARY or INTELLIGENCE SUMMARY

(Erase heading not required.)

DADOS 38th Divn

Place	Date	Hour	Summary of Events and Information	Remarks and references to Appendices
POPERINGHE	23		Two 4.5 Howitzers received. These have been on demand since 21st April and 3rd May respectively. One truck of winter clothing sent to Base. The town was lightly shelled today.	
	24		do.	
	25		Started withdrawal of 1st Blanket. The eleven limbered wagons G.S. complete turnouts, issued for Inf. Battalions for Lewis Guns arrived. A few shells were again fired into the town today. Visited wagon lines of 4 & 93/122.	
	26		Three 9.45" T.M's received; completing the establishment of 4 V/38 Heavy T.M Batty. Visited Div T.M.D. & 114 & 115 Bde M.G.	
	28		17. R.W.B. Sergt. DONALD A., A.O.C. 01886, (attached for instruction) left for duty with O.O. 2nd Anzac Corps Troops. Visited 113 Bde HQ. & 16 R.W.F. in reserve area HOUTKERKE. Three trucks (blankets) sent to Base today. The town was lightly shelled again. No station & loading operations were temporarily suspended.	
	29. 31		During the month the whole of the Lewis Guns of the 115 Brigade & 19th Welsh (Pioneer) Regt. and the Vickers Guns of the 115 Mn G. Coy were overhauled in the Divisional Armourers shop.	

J.H.Clifford Capt
DADOS 38 Divn.

31 May 1917.

WAR DIARY or INTELLIGENCE SUMMARY

Army Form C. 2118.

D.A.D.O.S. 38. Division

June 1917

Vol 19

Place	Date	Hour	Summary of Events and Information	Remarks and references to Appendices
POPERINGHE	June 2		Visited H.Q. 114 Inf. Brigade & C/122 R.F.A. wagon lines.	
	3		Railhead (POPERINGHE) was shelled this morning. No transport allowed in till after 11 a.m. Truck was then cleared, but not in time to issue to units at ration dump (RESELHOEK).	
	4		Railhead upon shell lightly in morning. Three trucks of winter clothing sent to Base.	
	5		Visited 130 Field Amb.e. Received 18 Pdr. Carriage demanded from 2nd A. Gun Park on 3rd.	
	7		"16th Welsh Regt. Transport lines. Town very lightly shelled in afternoon. One fell four yards from the stores & wrecked the men's toilet. No casualties.	
	8		Two trucks with stores arrived, but none arrived with the supply train. One truck Winter Clothing sent to Base.	
	10		Received one Vickers M.G. for 178 M.G. Coy.	
	11		Two 18 Pdr Guns and one Carriage received.	
	12		No truck arrived with supply train to-day. Divisional H.Q. moved to DRAGON Camp (A15.b.9 u. Sheet 28.) Division became part of XIV Corps to-day.	
DRAGON CAMP	13		A.D.O.S. XIV Corps visited new dump. Moved office & dump to a clearing in the woods at A.16.a.1.4t. (Sheet 28) in order to be nearer Div H.Q. and within the Divisional area. Demanded 4.5 How's carriage to replace "Premature".	
	14		Received one 2" T.M.	
	15		D.D.O.S. Fifth Army visited dump 1540 hrs.	
	16		Moved Armourers shop to A.16.a.1.4.	
	17		Demanded one 4.5 How's & carriage to replace another destroyed by "Premature".	
	19		Received one Lewis Gun for 10th S.W.B. and one 3" Stokes Mortar.	
	20		Visited 113 Brigade H.Q. (Canal Bank) & 113 In. G. Coy.	
	22		Received one 4.5 How. & carriage for D/122.	
	23		Railhead changed to INTERNATIONAL CORNER Station (A.2.d.9.1. Sheet 28.) See supply train failed to arrive there and Ordnance truck was cleared at POPERINGHE and stores	

WAR DIARY
INTELLIGENCE SUMMARY

(Erase heading not required.)

Army Form C. 2118.

D.A.D.O.S. 38th Division. June 1917.
contd.

Place	Date	Hour	Summary of Events and Information	Remarks and references to Appendices
DRAGON CAMP	28 June		issued to units at the newly arranged ration dumps later in the day.	
	25		Truck arrived at new Railhead today. One 18 Pdr gun received. Supplies were issued to the units direct from train and Ordnance Stores issued at same time.	
	28		Division started moving to Thiennes area in First Army. Railhead changed to CAESTRE. The truck of general Stores and two trucks containing machine gun personnel were not cleared owing to the fact that notification of charge of Railhead was not received in time. Received 3.6" mortar TMs	
	29		Moved with Divisional Headquarters to NORRENT FONTES in First Army. Turning over Railhead changed to AIRE, where the three trucks of stores recovered from CAESTRE were cleared today, and stores issued at specially arranged points in the afternoon. During the latter part of this month the Mobiles g[un]s of the four MG Coys carried out a very heavy shoot of importance firing and heavy demands for new barrels were received. Some difficulty was experienced owing to a shortage of supply of stores. There were also some delay in getting turning out spares for 18 Pdr guns; a few minor stores have been received & distributed viz the Divl Artillery such 2 Field Coys & Pioneer Batts. Remained 3 were a further 29 E Division MG Coy & from with we long were refer with 2nd & 29 E Division. Div	
NORRENT FONTES	30			

30/6/17

J. C. W[...] Capt.
D.A.D.O.S. 38 E Division.

D A Dir. Ordnance Service.   War Diary 38th.

1   1915

29/11/1915 Left Folkestone for Boulogne with advance party of 38th (W) Division.

July 1916.

3 Moved with DHQ to TREUX. Reserve of PH helmets with the exception of one 4000 which were taken with us, were left at LEAVILLERS during these 2 moves, and were brought to TREUX.

5 Railhead changed to MÉRICOURT sur L'Ancre. Div HQ to GROVETOWN. Ordnance remains at TREUX.

6 w/night The Div rel 7th in the front line of 2 Bdes of 2nf went into action at MAMETZ wood. One L/Gun reported destroyed.

10 Railhead changed to EDGEHILL

11 Div came out of line in the evening & DHQ returned to TREUX

Part leng 12 Div less Arty + one bde of Inf moved to Reserve Area. with HQ + Ordnance Dump at PONT REMY. To save transport damaged with relaying Div to exchange reserve of PH Helmets

13. Railhead changed to LONGPRÉ Visited all the IB HQs to ascertain important deficiencies in arms equipment + found that many losses of L/Guns + some M/G's had not been reported, so called for demands from all units. As a result a further 18 Lewis + 3 Vickers Guns were demanded from base.

The following shows net losses of these guns during the actions of 6 – 11th us.

	to replace n/r	to replace lost	Total	Salved + rep	Total Losses
LG	9	13	22	8	14
	3	n/	8	2	1
	12	13	25 / 10		15

Army Form C. 2118.

WAR DIARY
INTELLIGENCE SUMMARY
(Erase heading not required.)

D.A.D.O.S.
D.D.O.S. — 38th Division
July 1917

Place	Date	Hour	Summary of Events and Information	Remarks and references to Appendices
NORRENT FONTES	1		One truck of stores received today. Started overhaul of Vickers guns in Ord. Armourers Shop. Visited D.D.O.S. First Army and arranged for visit from the First Army Inspector of Armourers to advise as to the heavy wear noticed on the Vickers M. Guns.	
	2		Visited 115 Brigade H.Q. & 121 Field Amb.	
	3-10		Visiting units daily to ascertain that all deficiencies of mobilization equipment were on indent and that their requirements were being met satisfactorily. Completed the overhaul of Vickers guns of 114 & 115 Bde Coys in Ord Armourers Shop.	
	10		4.5 Hows. & carriage indented for on 13/6/17 received today. These were sent up to 38th Div D.A.D.O.S. to be handed over to unit.	
	11		Went to CALAIS to fetch some stores urgently required for the Divisional Train.	
	12-16		Visiting units. Completed the overhaul of Vickers Guns of 113 M.G. Coy. All guns (Vickers) of this Division had worn considerably by the heavy Barrage work recently done, and the check levers & buckstraps were in most cases badly worn & needing replacement.	
	17		Railhead changed to PROVEN. Sent lorries to clean rail head & dump stores in a tent pending arrival. Issues made to advanced Brigade Group Hq.	
PROVEN	18		Moved to PROVEN one day in advance of Div. H.Q. Issues made to those other units of the Division at their various refilling points.	
	19		Div. H.Q. arrived at PROVEN. Units commenced moving into the forward area of XIV Corps.	
	21		Railhead changed to INTERNATIONAL CORNER STATION. Div H.Q. moved to DRAGON Camp. Ordnance returning with them to former Dump at A.16.a.1.4 Sheet 28.	
DRAGON CAMP	22		Issued large quantities of special stores for coming Offensive viz Jackadders, ammunition & water carriers extra water bottles &c.	
	23		Visiting units as far as possible to ensure all were complete with equipment.	
	30		During this period there were large numbers of casualties in guns & mortars owing	

Army Form C. 2118.

WAR DIARY
INTELLIGENCE SUMMARY
(Erase heading not required.)

DADOS 38 Dn.   July 1917 (cont.)

Place	Date	Hour	Summary of Events and Information	Remarks and references to Appendices
DRAGON CAMP	23-30		to frequent raids by our Infantry, and the heavy firing constantly taking place. Five 18 Pdrs. Seven 2"TM's. One 3" Stokes, eight Lewis Guns and two Vickers Guns were replaced within 8 days.	
	30		All units now complete with their equipment with a few minor exceptions. All spare parts of machine & Lewis guns completed to establishment, and no gun, machine gun nor mortar was deficient. 340 Revolvers are still due to the Division. Were very nearly up for Lewis gunners & 178 for 3 Coy who are at present armed with rifles.	
	31		Division went into action today. All objectives gained. No reports of casualties to guns yet received. Issued tonight 39 sets of Pickerdilly to replace that lost in action.	

M.E. Wilmot Capt
DADOS. 38 Dn.

Army Form C. 2118.

WAR DIARY
INTELLIGENCE SUMMARY

D.A.D.O.S. 38th Div.

August 1917

Vol 21

Place	Date	Hour	Summary of Events and Information	Remarks and references to Appendices
DRAGON CAMP	1-3 Aug		Heavy reinforcements demanded during this period. Of machine guns & Lewis guns the 30 cwt lorry Company attached made several journeys daily to Gun Park and any rapid replacement was thereby made. Very heavy rain fell almost continuously, and consequently made demands for large supplies of clothing in anticipation of the withdrawal of the Division for Rest. The Brigade was moved out of the line to-day. He men were all wet through & covered with mud. All received a dry change of underclothing & SD clothing immediately. Visited Staff Captain who stated that considerable deficiencies of Equipment were being reported to him.	
	4			
	5, 6		Two Brigades withdrawn to reserve area near PROVEN	
	6		Div HQ moved to CENTRAL CAMP PROVEN (Ordnance dump moved to a field 1 mile to the South, at E.18.d.5.2. (Sheet 27)	
PROVEN	7		Railhead changed from to GRUBBEM. Completed to overhaul of the Lewis Guns of 17 & 115 Coy. & moved Armourer Shop to new position near PROVEY.	
	8, 15		Visited all the Infantry Brigade H.Q.s & Army units. Inspected re-fitting. Paid daily the Div: Salvage Dump and Corps Salvage Dump & had head to catting equipment & stores. Very heavy receipts from Base during the period most units were practically complete in stores except for certain articles, and no complaints pricto. A.O.G.s were overhauled in the Div. Armourers Shop.	
	17		All the Vickers Guns of the Force Brigade	

Army Form C. 2118.

WAR DIARY
or
INTELLIGENCE SUMMARY
(Erase heading not required.)

D.A.D.O.S. 38th Division

Aug '17 (cont)

Place	Date Aug	Hour	Summary of Events and Information	Remarks and references to Appendices
PROVEN	17		Demanded Nos. 18 Pln Q7s to replace others condemned for wear. Reported to Dist H.Q. the very excessive replacement of linen which have been made in certain important stores & equipment. Sent copy of report to the list of articles to A.D.O.S. XIV Corps for information. Railhead changed to INTERNATIONAL CORNER STATION.	
	18.			
	19.		Divisional HQ moved its advanced position at ELVERDINGHE CHATEAU and rear position at DRAGON CAMP. Ordnance stores moved to a position near its latter camp at A.9. central. Shut 28. Taking over position & stores from DADOS. 20th Divn.	
DRAGON CAMP	20		Demanded one 4.5 Howr & carriage to replace one destroyed by enemy fire. one in replacement of one condemned for wear. Demanded on 18th Pln Q7s to replace one destroyed by enemy fire. one 15 Pdr Q7 & carriage (promotive.)	
	21			
	23		Visited Gun Park (Fifth Army) reference difficulty in getting spare parts by pillar levers reported deficiencies to A.O.S. XIV Corps.	
	26			
	27 – 31st		Very rainy weather during this period and in consequence received rather heavy demands for clothing etc from Brigade in front line. Stores generally during the month came out very well & there were no serious shortages of anything.	

31/8/17

N Clifford Capt
D A D O S 38 Divn

Army Form C. 2118.

Sept 1917

D.A.D.O.S.
38th Division

Vol 22

WAR DIARY
INTELLIGENCE SUMMARY
(Erase heading not required.)

Place	Date Sept	Hour	Summary of Events and Information	Remarks and references to Appendices
DRAGON CAMP (28/1.9 Cent)	1-4		Waiting rants, Salvage dumps. J.O.M. A.D.O.S. XIV Corps & D.A.D.O.S. 20th Div.	
	5		Went to SAILLY to see D.A.D.O.S. 57th Div. reference coming take over from him.	
	6		Demanded one Vickers Gun & to replace one destroyed, also one 18 Pdr Q.F. Gun & 1/12.1 R.F.A.	
	7		Telegraphed CALAIS Base to cease issues after today.	
	8		Received last consignments of stores from W. Base.	
	9		Hand over arrangements to new area commenced. 115 Brigade moved into PROVEN area.	
	10		Telegraphed to S. Base HAVRE to issue stores on 12th as that first supplies may be received on 14th inst. Div HQ moved to ROUEN for Clothing, etc.	
	11		Div HQ moved to PROVEN. Railhead changed to GRUBBERN. Div Ordnance did not move.	
	12		Returned large quantities of special stores to O.O. XIV Corps Dumps i.e. Packsaddlery water carriers, Emergency ammunition carriers, winter Moths, Apron packs etc which had been withdrawn from units during last 3 days.	
BAC ST MAUR	13		Ordnance moved to BAC ST MAUR to temporary Camp in field adjoining my dump of D.A.D.O.S. 57th Div. Handed over special stores to D.A.D.O.S. 57th Div. Railhead changed to CAESTRE. Stores from HAVRE & ROUEN did not arrive.	
	14		Visited A.D.O.S. XI Corps.	
	15		Visited D.O.M. XI Corps at HAZEBROUCK. Ordnance Workshop (Light); also XI Corps Laundry.	
	16		Railhead changed to LA GORGUE. Cleared two dumps of stores one each from HAVRE & ROUEN. Attached units of 57th Div. transferred for Ordnance to 38th Div.	
	17		Divisional H.Q. moved to CROIX DU BAC. Ordnance moved into the office	

Army Form C. 2118.

WAR DIARY or INTELLIGENCE SUMMARY

(Erase heading not required.)

Place	Date	Hour	Summary of Events and Information	Remarks and references to Appendices
DAC ST MAUR	17		and buildings occupied previously by D.A.D.O.S. 57th Division, at G.18.C.5.8. sheet 36, and both over surplus & area stores.	
	18		No stores received today.	
	19		Stores obtained from HAIKE & ROVEN ah 21 trenches. Capt. B CLIFFORD departed for 10 days leave to ENGLAND. Major H. EARDLEY-WILMOT DARMC. 38 Div. answering for him whilst absent.	
	20		38 Divisional Artillery relieved the 57th Divisional Artillery in the lines	
	22		One truck of general stores received on 20th.	
	23		Three truckes of stores received today.	
	24		One truck of general stores received	
	25		No limbers arrived. Three truck were advised yesterday	
	26		Four truck trucks advised today.	
	27		One truck of stores received	
	29		Capt. CLIFFORD returned to duty today. Seven trucks of stores received containing hays horse and N.C containers for Box respirators. All units received the latter. To complete the exchange for old pattern & salt bags.	
	30		Five trucks of stores today, containing remainder of Horse rugs & pair of unit blankets. Stores were received very irregularly from these during latter part of month but no return or experiences who caused from 13th to 30th 8 Pensioners were evacuated daily in Sick Ammunition ship.	

Mellon Capt
D.A.D.O.S. 38 Div

WAR DIARY

INTELLIGENCE SUMMARY
(Erase heading not required.)

Army Form C. 2118.

D.A.D.O.S. 38th Divn.

October 1917.

Vol 23

Place	Date	Hour	Summary of Events and Information	Remarks and references to Appendices
BAC ST MAUR	Oct 1		A.D.O.S. XI Corps visited the dump & inspected workshops etc.	
	2		Went to ARMENTIERES in accordance with orders from "Q" to requisition forges and anvils etc for use in the Divisional Forge now being started. First Army inspected the office stores & workshops.	D.D.O.S. inspected
	3		First trucks of stores received from including the "first blanket" for whole of Division. The majority of the blankets being issued the same day.	
	5		The First Army Inspector of Armourers inspected the Divisional Shop, being of the opinion that more armourers should be withdrawn for work here. (only 6 at present 2 left)	
	6		Truck of stores due but did not arrive. Visited First Army Heavy Mobile Workshop, also the Gun Park to fetch some urgently required stores. Visited items received at 2 a.m. today. No truck arrived, another advised as due today.	
	7		One truck of stores received.	
	8		Three trucks of stores at Railhead - too much to move to dump at return dump.	
	10		Divisional Forge completed & started no making old horseshoes serviceable. Carrier Sergt & men showing smiths withdrawn from units of the Division.	
			A.A. & Q.M.G. inspected the Ordnance Depot, workshops etc. Accompanied one to L.Park from Gun Park. No trucks of stores from Base Park.	
	12		Visited A.D.O.S. and Dept A. Gen. Rols. No truck received today.	
	14		Three days issues of General stores received to-day. Also 1000 Gum boots thigh sent to Sergeis Stores. Capt. RICHARDS, 13 Welsh Regt. attached for 3 days instruction.	
	15		Another truck Gum Boots thigh received today.	
	16		No trucks at Rail head this morning. Eight trucks advised at 2pm as being at LA GORGUE. These left Base at 4pm. Three of these — containing general stores	

WAR DIARY or INTELLIGENCE SUMMARY

Army Form C. 2118.

(Erase heading not required.)

Instructions regarding War Diaries and Intelligence Summaries are contained in F.S. Regs., Part II. and the Staff Manual respectively. Title Pages will be prepared in manuscript.

2 ADOS 35 Div.

Oct. 17/cont.

Place	Date	Hour	Summary of Events and Information	Remarks and references to Appendices
BAC ST MAUR.	18		About 1000 Gum Boots were cleaned, the others containing blankets were left to be sent on to Divisional Rest Camp during the night.	
	19		Cleared 600 Trucks - 5 Blankets, 1 ground sheet - Issued the usual blankets to all units	
	20		1500 Gum Boots kept moist. Remained on 18th R.P. to replace one contained in escort heading over to the Stores Infants Purpose H.Q.	
	21			
	22		These 35th Stores Burdon demanded an replenishment of stores damaged shell fire. No others received for three days from Base.	
	23		Fur Trucks Patries at R.H. today, including 100 hot pots contained + 400 Brasiers	
	24		Demanded Lewis Gun Jar 105 WTS to 24/Run on Antwerped & received it from Sun Park namely 26	
	25		Received 1500 Gum Boots 27/10, completing to 7500 authorised for the Division.	
	26		Night "PB" men arrived from ETAPLES this evening for attachment, & ultimately to be places 2 Clerks & 6 Storemen AOC (category A)	
	27		Capt R. JONES 13 R.W.F. attached for 3 days instruction. Inspected & examined the 8 P.B. men. Found them entirely unsuitable for Ordnance duties & only one of them possible for training as a clerk. They are all wounded or otherwise unfit men from Scotch Infantry Battns.	
	28		Visited DDOS Third Army reference exchange of some of the P.B. men for more suitable ones. Went to the Gun Park & Heavy Stores Workshop.	
	29		Met with DAQMG & Third Army H.Q. Workshop. More Trucks of stores attached to Army at LA GORGUE at 3 p.m. Sent lorries to cleared 2 of them. Others sent to Div. Railhead at night	
	30		Cleared 8 Trucks of stores today, containing Gutta 73 Boots Blankets & general stores	
	31		Issued all the Gutta to Infantry and the majority of the D.S. Boots. Stores were received very irregularly from Base during the month. Have arriving for several days in succession & then several Trucks at one time so that the system of delivering daily to units at Railhead could not be carried out. Completed overhaul of Lewis Guns in Div. Lewis Shop.	

31/10/17

M.C. Wright Capt.
ADOS 35 Div.

Army Form C. 2118.

D.A.D.O.S. 38th Division
November 1917

WAR DIARY
INTELLIGENCE SUMMARY.
(Erase heading not required.)

Place	Date	Hour	Summary of Events and Information	Remarks and references to Appendices
BAC ST MAUR	Nov. 1917			
	1		Demanded one 3" Stokes for 115 T.M.B. to replace one destroyed shell-fire.	
	2		One A.T. 18 Pdr condemned for scoring & replacement demanded.	
	3		G.O.C. & A.A.&Q.M.G inspected stores, workshops etc.	
	4		Received two 3" Stokes Mortars demanded on 23/10 & 24/10 respectively.	
	5		Visited First Army Gun Park to obtain stores urgently required, also Brit. Wimberley Road.	
	7		Received one Vickers Br.G demanded on 5th	
	9		Visited H.Q. 122 Bde R.F.A. also 114 Inf Bde H.Q. & transport-lines of 15 Welsh Regt.	
	11		Visited wagon lines of two batteries of 121 Bde to enquire into excessive demands	
			I went to the gun position of C. Battery to see the O.C. Battery	
	13		Visited all regimental boot shops of 113 Bde reference complaint as to bad quality of boots recently issued. Obtained samples of these & sent them to base for inspection	
			A.D.V.S. II Corps inspected the Divisional Forge. also Bn. Workshops in Stores	
	14		Capt. B. CLIFFORD left for No 14 But. Depot to take a course in Ammunition for Wastage. Lt. McROBIE of the Divisional armoury for this W.O. duty.	
	15		Received two 3" Stokes demanded on 1/11 in replacement of I destroyed shell-fire.	
	17		Received four 18 Pdrs. from Gun Park for 147 AFA Bde. Recently joined the Divn.	

Army Form C. 2118.

WAR DIARY
INTELLIGENCE SUMMARY.
(Erase heading not required.)

D.A.D.O.S
38 Div
Nov (cont)
1917

Place	Date	Hour	Summary of Events and Information	Remarks and references to Appendices
BAC ST MAUR	Nov. 20		97 18 Pdr demanded on 22nd Rept received today.	
	21		A.D.O.S XI Corps with G.A.D.O.S XI Corps visited classes & workshops.	
	22		Came under administration of XI Corps today. One move of XI Corps to Italy.	
			One A.D.C. steamer sent to I.B.D. Today an ordinary steamer to Infantry.	
	26		Received one Lewis Gun No 10 F. S.W.Rs. to replace one destroyed by shellfire.	
	28		All orders for 18 Pdrs & 4.5 Hows outstanding to units were cancelled today on instructions of First Army. Actual deficiencies were obtained and fresh indents submitted viz. One 18 Pdr Carriage for C/121, one 4.5 How for D/121, One 18 Pdr for 97 Batty, and aim 4.5 Hows for C/332 Bde R.F.A.	
	30		Capt J.C. LIPPARD returned from duty as O.C the Adv. Ordnance Depot ZENINGHEM. During the month returns have been received very irregularly from Bacs. Knew services taking up 5 days on route. All the Pickers Guns of the from 3 Machine Gun Companies together with mountings & spare parts have been returned to Divisional Armourers Shop.	

30/11/1917.

W.C.Williams Capt
D.A.D.O.S 38 Div

Army Form C. 2118.

P.A.D.O.S.
38th Division
December 1917

WAR DIARY
INTELLIGENCE SUMMARY.
(Erase heading not required.)

Place	Date	Hour	Summary of Events and Information	Remarks and references to Appendices
BAC ST MAUR	1		Three N.C.O. Storemen (Category A) left for transfer to Infantry Base depot.	
	2		Visited No 12 Ord. M. Workshop reference 6" T.M. emplacements required.	
	3		" HQ 113 Inf. Bde & 115 Inf. Bde also 113 Machine Gun Company.	
	5		On 4/5 Hour for D/121 dispatched on 29/11/17 received today.	
	7		Visited A Battery 147 A.F.A. Bde reference disposal of pivot sights & cam of hamers.	
	9		115 Inf. Bde turned into Reserve area. Stated verbal of their trenching in Quiet Armourer's Shop. Visited Heavy Mobile Workshop installation on DADOS Test Army.	
	10		Visited S.XT Corps and R.D.V.S. XT Corps inspected Divisional toys. Visited Brigade School. 114 Inf. Bde also 15 Welsh Regt reference supply of Cap's provision.	
	11		Visited 121 M.G. Bn & 123 M.G. Bn also 113 Bde M.B.	
	12		Received one 3" Stokes T.M. for 115 T.M. B5. Demanded one 18 Pdr Q.F. gun for B/113 to replace one with Ivat-breech ring caused by detonation of Artillery charge.	
	14		Three "P.B." personnel (surplus to requirements) transferred forts, in accordance with orders received from third Army.	
	16		Received notification of funding charge of Base. C.R.O.S. XT Corps called in afternoon.	

Army Form C. 2118.

D.A.D.O.S.
38 Division.

Dec 1917 (cont.)

WAR DIARY
INTELLIGENCE SUMMARY.
(Erase heading not required.)

Instructions regarding War Diaries and Intelligence Summaries are contained in F. S. Regs., Part II. and the Staff Manual respectively. Title pages will be prepared in manuscript.

Place	Date	Hour	Summary of Events and Information	Remarks and references to Appendices
BAC ST MAUR	Dec 14		Captain A.H. WILKINS. 11th South Wales Borderers attached for 3 days instruction Base. charged to CALAIS. Last truck with Ordnance stores for this Division left the Base.	
	19		HAVRE today. Received 2 3" Stokes T.M's.	
	20		Attended conference at Corps H.Q. to discuss means of improving the organization for collection of Salvage. Received 3. 18 Pdr R7 guns in replacement of others worn.	
	22		Obtained 5 lewis guns from 20 Corps Troops & issued them to P.B. personnel in charge of Ammunition dumps in back areas, and withdrew the 5 Pre issued lorries to them by 19th (Division) Welsh Regt. Visited Divl Bomb stores.	
	24		Cancelled indents for 5. 4.5 Howitzers (condemned for wear) authorty First Army O.S. 9520 d. 29/11/17	
	25		Two 3" Stokes T.M's received for 115 Pn S Coy. also 1 Vickers P.G. for 113 Pn. S. Coy.	
	27		Visited First Army Gun Park to get air recuperator pumps urgently required for new 18 Pdr guns recently taken over from 3rd Portuguese Divn.	
	28		Issued 113 & 114 Inf Bde HQ. also Bde Bomb stores	
	31		Received 1 18 Pdr Q7 gun for C/122 R.F.A. also two 3" Stokes T.M's for 115 T.M Battery. Very severe frost for past few days in consequent heavy demands for frost cogs & nails. Units state the frozen quickly wear away & are easily broken off on the hard roads.	

W.M.Moncrieff
D.A.D.O.S. 38 Divn

Army Form C. 2118.

WAR DIARY
INTELLIGENCE SUMMARY
(Erase heading not required.)

D.A.D.O.S. 38th Division
May 1918.
Vol 30

Place	Date	Hour	Summary of Events and Information	Remarks and references to Appendices
TOUTENCOURT	May 1.		D.D.O.S. First Army, with A.D.O.S. V Corps called and inspected Office, dump and the Workshops. Returned 1 truck Winter Clothing (Jerkins etc) to Railhead ROSEL.	M. 36. a. (Sheet 57 D)
	2.		Went to DOMQUEUR with A.A. & Q.M.G. to visit Divisional Re-inforcement Wing and arrange for supplies of Ordnance Stores to them and to the "Battle Surplus". (Total about 2,200 men, 150 Officers)	
	3.		Railhead changed to BELLE EGLISE. Supply trains had to be cleaned by 4 a.m. Re-filling at 6 a.m.	
	4.		Visited OO V Corps Dumps at MAURS, reference some urgently required stores. Visited Salvage Dump.	
	6.		Divl. HQrs moved to TOUTENCOURT. Went to ABBEVILLE to obtain white calico for special operations. Purchased 206 metres. Unable to get this at Ord Depot. no purchased under orders from G.O.C. required immediately.	authority 38 Div Q 6793 dated 6·5·18
	7.		Visited ROSEL to arrange for return of more Winter Clothing. Attended Court of Enquiry at 114 Bde HQrs. HARPONVILLE — hrenching 3" clothes with No 146 Forge. No evidence obtainable as to cause.	
	8.		Received orders that Railhead must be cleaned by 4 a.m. Issued stores at re-filling points at 6 a.m. Visited Baths at HARPONVILLE + inspected system of exchange of underclothing. Inspected also Divisional Clothing exchange for gas cases. 200 complete changes of S.B. Clothing + underclothing in stock.	
	9.		Rail-head had to be cleared at 2 a.m. today. As refilling was at an uncertain time after this + no representatives of units were present Ordnance Stores were taken back to Dump for splitting up + issues made as units called later in the day. Arranged with D.A.D.O.S. 12th Division to fill no truck conjointly with Winter Clothing (Jerkins etc). Visited Salvage Dump.	

Army Form C. 2118.

WAR DIARY
or
INTELLIGENCE SUMMARY.
(Erase heading not required.)

Instructions regarding War Diaries and Intelligence Summaries are contained in F. S. Regs., Part II. and the Staff Manual respectively. Title pages will be prepared in manuscript.

Place	Date	Hour	Summary of Events and Information	Remarks and references to Appendices
TOUTENCOURT	May 10		One G.S limbered Wagon, complete turn out, arrived today for Divl. Signal Coy. Visited I.O.M. 46.O.M.W.(L) to arrange that cylinder Stanton lorry, requiring recharging could be sent to him. Is to go in his lorry to I.O.3. O.M.W.(H) to save transport. Zero Battalion of 114 Bde in action this morning at AVELUY WOOD. Objectives not obtained.	
	11.		Visited Staff Captain 114 Bde to obtain information of any lorries of guns etc. Town reported yet. Cleared Railhead at 3. a.m. 89 Hd. food Containers received & issued. Visited Salvage Dump & sent lorries to clear this loads to Railhead.	
	12		Went to C.O. I Corps troops to obtain S.B. Clothing & arrange collection of underclothing which he had for disposal. Issued 120 suits of S.B Clothing to B. Coy. 38 M.G. Battn who were being withdrawn from line with men in a "lousy" state. The "Foden" Disinfector had been sent to workshops for inspection & was not available. Infected clothing will be treated & re issued. Visited the Divisional Baths at HARPONVILLE and HÉDAUVILLE, and also Salvage Dump.	
	13.		Attended Railhead and Salvage Dump. A.D.O.S. I Corps inspected Officers, Sergs and workshops. Inspected Qr Mrs Stores of 13th R.W.F. and 15th R.W.F.; also the Batts Boot & Tailors Shops.	
	14		Railhead at 4.a.m. Supply train was 3 hours late owing to jam. Visited 159 Field Ambce. Salvage Dump & Ammunition Railhead, PUCHEVILLERS. Received one T.M. (Stokes) for 115 T.M.Batty.	

Army Form C. 2118.

WAR DIARY
or
INTELLIGENCE SUMMARY.
(Erase heading not required.)

D.A.D.O.S
38th Division
May 1918

Place	Date	Hour	Summary of Events and Information	Remarks and references to Appendices
TOUTENCOURT.	May 15.		Visited 38th Div. Reinforcement Wing at MAISON PONTHIEU reference supplies of Ordnance Stores & their method of accounting for them; as details of all Battalions (i.e. Battle Surplus) are with them & constantly being changed. Visited also 3rd Army Sniping, Obs., & Scouting School ref. supply of telescopic rifles. 03831. Pte HYDE.A. Storeman A.O.C. reported for duty to fill vacancy on A.O.C. staff.	
	16.		Attended Railhead and Salvage Dump. Visited O.C. Div. Sniping Coy.	
	17.		Visited 114 & 115 Inf. Bde. H.Qs. also Qr. Mrs. stores of 13th, 14th, R.W. Fus. and 13th/14th & 15th Welsh Regt. On usual visit to Div. H.Q. "Q" enquired why I would not supply varnish for use on transport vehicles & considered that such should be obtained. I stated that sufficient paint was always available, that varnish was not allowed for this purpose, and that as it was not an essential it should not be purchased. I was told that some must be obtained quickly.	
	18.		The 38th Div. Artillery arrived in Third Army area. Received "move order" for Ordnance supply from by this Division. from II Corps troops. General confirmation of move to all concerned. Borrowed four 18Pdr. Guns, one 18Pdr. carriage, and one 4.5 How. & carriage from No 3 Gun Park.	
	19.		Purchased 25 litres Varnish, and received orders to supply enough for "all wagons of the Division" (antony) (R.62 at 1/5 A.D.O.S. V Corps called. Reported orders ref. Varnish supply to him & was instructed not to purchase any more without Third Army approval. Wrote letter to A.D.O.S. asking for later approval for local purchase or for supply from Base.	

Army Form C. 2118.

A.D.O.S. 38 Div.

WAR DIARY
or
INTELLIGENCE SUMMARY.
(Erase heading not required.)

May 1918 (cont'd)

Place	Date	Hour	Summary of Events and Information	Remarks and references to Appendices
TOUTENCOURT	May 19		A.O.C. Personnel, 1 W.O., 1 Clerk & 1 Storeman with one lorry rejoined from O.O. II Corps Tps. Having been detached for duty with the Divisional Artillery.	
	20.		Received H.Q. 18 Pdr guns & 1 carriage; also 1 4.5 How'r & carriage demanded on 18th. Visited H.Q. 38 Div. Artillery at MONPLAISIR reference deficiencies in equipment & to arrange about supplies. Demanded 1 18 Pdr gun & two carriages in replacement of some left in 2nd Army.	
"	20.		Relief of Division in line by 35th Division completed. Div H.Q. moved to HERISSART. Cleared new Rail head - ROSEL - at 10 a.m. & moved stores at re-filling points. Visited 115 Bde. H.Q. & took Staff Capt. with me to see O.C. 2nd R.W.F. reference excessive demands for S.D. Clothing. 211st Army	
	21		Two trucks Stores advised, but failed to arrive at Rail head. Lorries returned empty. Visited J.D.M.	
	22		46 D.A.W.(L.) reference issue of new guns & return of the unserviceable to Base.	
	23.		Three trucks of Stores at Rail head today. Cleared two & made issues at re-filling points. Lorries returned late & cleared the third bringing the stores back to the Dump. Attended Artillery Refilling front at GEZAINCOURT. Visited 203 Coy. Div. Train & A & B Batteries 121 Bde R.F.A.	
	24		One truck load of winter clothing (under clothing) returned to Orn today. Overhaul of all Lewis Guns of 115 Bde in Bde Armr Shop at rate of 12 per day commenced.	
	25		Visited H.Q. 113 Bde & Qr Stores of two Battalions in RUBEMPRE & received complaints of quality & front (recently issued) for Steel Helmets that the enamel would not attach to it, & came steel one	

WAR DIARY or INTELLIGENCE SUMMARY

Army Form C. 2118.

D.A.D.O.S. 35th Div.

May 1918 (Cont'd)

Place	Date	Hour	Summary of Events and Information	Remarks and references to Appendices
TOUTENCOURT	May 25.		was the case. Found that paint was not as normally issued & wrote Base concerning it. Returned one truck White Clothing - (underclothing) to Base.	
	26.		Truck of Clothing from ROUEN failed to arrive. Obtained more that was urgently required from DADOS 36 Div. Received 36 Lewis Guns complete, to each up Battalion to 24 each. Examined all in Div. Armt Shop before issue, as cases of undue tightness of fitting has been noticeable recently. Received one 18 Pdr. Q.F. gun.	
	27.		90 stores at Railhead. Though one truck advised & lorries had useless journey. Visited 9.0.M. No. 46 D.M.W.(L) ref return of BM's of 18 Pdrs recently replaced. Saw also O.C. No 3 Gun Park. Reference deficiencies ~~debits~~ of spare parts in charts of the Lewis Guns received yesterday.	
	28.		Two trucks now due at Railhead, none arrived again. Obtained some S.D. Clothing urgently required for Corps Commander's inspection tomorrow from D.O. Corps Tps. Visited Staff Capt 114th Bde & also O.C. 13 Welsh Regt. & saw the latter Battalion on Parade, noticing many deficiencies of equipment which were not due on indents reporting same to O.C.	
	29.		Two trucks of stores received today. Quantities were too great to be cleared by the four lorries, so one ~~truck~~ lorry load was taken to each refilling point & lorries returned to Railhead later & brought the stores which had been dumped at Railhead, back to the 35th Div'n Sp for distribution tomorrow. Visited 113 Bde. H.Q.	

Army Form C. 2118.

D.A.D.O.S
38 Div.
May 1918

WAR DIARY
or
INTELLIGENCE SUMMARY.
(Erase heading not required.)

Place	Date	Hour	Summary of Events and Information	Remarks and references to Appendices
TOUTENCOURT	May 30		Returned remaining odd lots of Winter Clothing. Withdrawal of all Winter Clothing except 1 pr Blanket, now completed. Drew 20 Snipers Rifles 1914 Patt from 3rd Army S.O.S. Depot. Railhead changed to CANDAS. Sent two lorries with stores direct to Artillery groups at BEAUNCOURT. Found all had moved to RAINCHEVAL, the notification of move not reaching me in time. Closed all stores later in day at RAINCHEVAL. Saw the moderation of 113 Brigade Group by Corps Commander. Visited Divisional & Corps Salvage Dumps.	
	31.			

HCWM Capt
D.A.D.O.S 38 Div.

WAR DIARY or INTELLIGENCE SUMMARY

Army Form C. 2118.

D.A.D.O.S. 38th Division

June 1918

Vol 31

Place	Date	Hour	Summary of Events and Information	Remarks and references to Appendices
TOUTENCOURT	June 1		Started with drawal of 1st Blankets. Visited Staff Capt. R.A. reference continued re-equipping demands from RA units & to hasten completion.	N.36.a. (Sheet 57 D)
	2		Visited A.D.O.S. 5 Corps, ref. re-crediting Surplus account with cwt of Varnish, as Div HQ had not received any order about it. Visited 2. R.W.F. reference excessive demands for S.D. Clothing. Sent 2 truck loads of Blankets to Base.	
	3		Attended Rail Head (CANDAS) with 4 Lorries. The truck arrived from ROUEN failed to arrive. Visited 115 Bde H.Q. and No 2 Coy Div Train. Transport Lines, also Salvage dump. Rail head changed to CANAPLES. Lorries took returned Ord. Stores for Base but were unable to load there & did so at VIGNACOURT & then cleared dumps at CANAPLES.	
	4		Divisional H.Q. moved to LEALVILLERS on completion of relief of 63rd Division in the line. Entrance Office did not move. Cleared heavy truck of stores from CANAPLES. Unable to send unwanted clothing to returned Ord. Stores to Base as Rail head could not accept.	O. 22. d. 1. b.
	6		Visited Artillery Wagon Lines. Wrote to Staff Capt. 38 Div R.A. hastening the providing of indents to complete the re-equipping as found many demands had not been sent in. Visited the Div Salvage Dumps, Div Baths & Exchange for gained clothing. Also I.O.M. O.Vn.10.(L) R.9/db reference vehicle repairs. Received one Vickers M.G. Visited A.R.P.	

Army Form C. 2118.

D.A.D.O.S.
38th (Welsh) Div.
June 1918

WAR DIARY
or
INTELLIGENCE SUMMARY
(Erase heading not required.)

Place	Date	Hour	Summary of Events and Information	Remarks and references to Appendices
TOUTENCOURT	8		D.D.O.S. Third Army and A.D.O.S. V Corps inspected Offices & Dump. No trucks from Base today.	
	9		One truck stores cleared from CAMPAGNES. Received train 15Ph. guns for A/122 Bde.	
	10		Rail head changed to CANDAS. S.O.M. (2nd 19/46 D.M.W. (L)) attended at dump to inspect vehicles of this Division requiring repair.	
	11		Railhead now able to accept stores for return to Base. Sent 1 truck load of Blankets.	
	12		Two trucks of stores at Rail head today. Unable to clear all in time for issue at Supply refilling point. Received one 15Ph gun & one 18Ph Carriage Limber for A/122.	
	13		Demanded additional 4 Lewis guns per Battalion. Sent to AUXI LE CHATEAU with several repairable telescopic rifles to Third Army S.O.O. Safety Short. Purchased special stores (electric torches) for coming operation.	
	14		Received 36 Lewis Guns for issue 4 each to Battalions, completing them to 28 per battalion exclusive of AA guns and of 4 guns each for AA work. All guns overhauled in Brig. Armrs Shop before issue. Visited 17 Hd.Qr., Gr.Hd., Stores & transport lines, also Salvage dumps at LEAVILLERS and VARENNES.	
	16		Demanded 15Ph carriage for C/122. Visited 130 Field Ambulance re transport issues of 10 SWB.	
	17		Inspected Salvage dump & examined Rabed Ammunition prior to sending to Rail head. Received one 15Ph gun and one 15Ph carriage, also 1 Vickers M.G.	
	19		Visited H.Q. Sig. Divin. reference Headlines for stores, also HQ D.A.C. reference heavy demands from the return for harness.	

Army Form C. 2118.

WAR DIARY or **INTELLIGENCE SUMMARY.**

(Erase heading not required.)

D.A.D.O.S. 38th Division.

June 1918

Place	Date	Hour	Summary of Events and Information	Remarks and references to Appendices
TOUTENCOURT	June 20		One lorry deficient today. M.T. Coy unable to supply replacement. Had difficulty in clearing railhead in time for issuing at re-filling points. D.D.O.S. & A.D.O.S. visited dump. Visited 9th Battalion R.E. stores & workshops, also 19th Welsh Reg. (Pioneers) transport lines.	
	21		Received one Ammunition wagon limber for 6/121, replace destroyed by shell fire. Inspected Ammunition refilling point with A.D.O.S. V Corps, also the ammunition in all sections of D.A.C. and the Divisional Grenade store.	
	22		Attended at Railhead - One Truck Special stores. No pack service colour was received though nearly 1 Ton was due. Reported same to Div. H.Q.	
	23		Two Trucks stores at Railhead. Unable to issue whole quantity at the filling points, as one truck was dumped for distribution next day. Visited Staff Captains of 113 & 114 Inf. Bdes.	
	~~24~~		87 Boots, ankle received from Base today. 90% were repaired nos. Reported this to A.D.O.S. as Infantry units complain about them as unsuitable for forward area. Received 1 18 Pdr 47, & 1 Vickers M.G.	
	24		Visited H.Q. of Div. Inf. & Bdes. reference apparent bad treatment of a gun. Visited Salvage Dump and Gun Stores of 16 RWF. Received 1 18 Pdr gun for B/122.	
	25		Visited wagon lines of 1 Sec D.A.C. and B/121 Bde. & inspected ammunition in limbers & wagons. Also greatcoats & ammunition stores. Received 1 Lewis gun for 2nd RWF. re-place one destroyed by shell fire.	

Army Form C. 2118.

WAR DIARY
or
INTELLIGENCE SUMMARY.
(Erase heading not required.)

D.A.D.O.S.
38th Division
June 1918.

Instructions regarding War Diaries and Intelligence Summaries are contained in F. S. Regs., Part II. and the Staff Manual respectively. Title pages will be prepared in manuscript.

Place	Date	Hour	Summary of Events and Information	Remarks and references to Appendices
	June			
TOUTENCOURT	26		Visited Transport Lines of 13th & 14th R.W.F. reference some large demands for Transport equipment. Inspected unfixed ammunition at Divl Salvage Dump, prior to being sent to Ammunition Refill Point. Attended Rail Head. No Service Colour Paint received again today. Visited Transport Lines of	
	27		2nd & 17th R.W.F. and inspected workshops & R.R. Stores. Found detailed parades & another Frank sterd at the former place & reported same to Bde HQ.	
	28		Visited A.D.O.S. V Corps re. disposal of Magazines L.G. ordered by Div HQ. to be returned home — 24 per Levis Guns from all Battalions. Called at OO I Corps Lmps for clerks, also Salvage Dump. Inspected Brigades etc at Divl Bomb Store. Visited Div Reception Camp and 131 Field Amb.	
	29.		Saw Staff Capt. R.A. reference the return of Harness Saddling from Batteries & ORE consignment on the recent reduction in Horses. Visited Divl Amm. Refilling Point with Staff Capt R.A. and inspected recent improvements suggested by A.D.O.S. on recent visit. Drew two 18-Pdr carriages from G.R. at AUXI LE CHATEAU & delivered them to 2.O.M. & 19/14 D.M.W.M.).	
	30		Stores from Base arrived irregularly during the month, sometimes 3 or 4 days overdue but no notizable lack of supply other than Paint, Service colour.	

J.W. [signature]
Major
D.A.D.S., 38th (Welsh) Division

Army Form C. 2118.

WAR DIARY
or
INTELLIGENCE SUMMARY.
(Erase heading not required.)

D.A.D.O.S. 38th Division.

July 1918.

JM 32

Place	Date	Hour	Summary of Events and Information	Remarks and references to Appendices
TOUTENCOURT	July 1918 1.		Visited wagon lines of D/121 & C/121 & examined the ammunition on the limbered wagons. Inspected B/m Stores. Visited Salvage Dump & sent lorry to clear stores received from there.	
	2.		Received 18 Pdr. B.F. for B/121. Went to MAGURS. Went to see O.O. E Corps Dps O/P from O.C. 9/A. Tps.	
	3.		Attended Rail Head. Sent lorries of returns to be cleared, borrowed one extra lorry from M.T. Coy for the purpose. Visited transport lines of 123 & 1344 Field Coys R.E.	
	4.		Received 8000 rds ammunition & returned to Dupt. Bakery Officer. This was necessary on account of the oven burning at ABBEVILLE being unable to exchange purchased working in others for ability received. Cont. FR. Worn A.D.C. Dept. for one months duty at HAVRE. Visit Depot. On probation for a commission. Visited Bomb Stk. No 3 Inf. Discrepancies in stores received & enquired as to where come from. Instructed for the Enno Jm to complete Battalion "E" scale G. i.e. 32 pr Batts exchange of 18 pr M.	
	6.		Attended Rail Hd. One truck of Clothing etc from ROUEN. Visited Transport lines of 124 & 151 Field Coys R.E. Investigated canvas of defective draught poles for lost carts. Received 36 Lewis Guns & passed them through Div Armourers shop for examination before issuing them tomorrow to Battalions.	
	7.		One truck from HAVRE today. Only received 12½% of service Point demanded. Visited H.Q. 122 Bde F.D.A. I saw the Colonel in command, Visited also 114 Bde (Inf) seeing both the G.O.C. & Staff Captain. I also went to Battery position of B/121 to see OC. reference delay in receipt of apen from J.O.M., & to see his A.A. Lewis Guns & the ammunition (a.p.m.) in the gun pits. Called at Div Salvage Dump at VARENNES.	

Army Form C. 2118.

WAR DIARY or INTELLIGENCE SUMMARY.
(Erase heading not required.)

D.A.D.O.S.
38th Div.

July 1918

Place	Date	Hour	Summary of Events and Information	Remarks and references to Appendices
TOUTENCOURT	July 8		Visited H.Q. of 113 & 115 Inf. Brigades, & 121 Bde. R.F.A. Observed that a portion of area occupied by units of the former was not clear of Salvage & reported same to Staff Capt. Rec'd One W.S. Hut for D/ers.	
	9.		Went to HESDIN to get information as to obtaining the increased transport authorised for H. Q. Batteries, & other matters, from the D.D.O.S. Third Army. — A.D.O.S. V Corps being on leave.	
	10.		Received one Rifle Gun for A/122. Visited Transport lines of H.Q. Coy. Div. Train. Received 1. Vickers Gun for 38. M.G. Battn. A.D.C. personnel — 1 N.C.O. & 1 Pte. — reported for duty at A.R.P. as instructed by Corps.	
	11		Visited A.R.P. to see new personnel & inspected the arrangements for sorting & stacking the ammunition & the sorting & stacking of empties. Attended distribution of stores at Ration dumps. Visited Salvage Dump.	
	12.		At Rail head. (D.A.D.O.S) One truck of stores from HAVRE., including 3rd of total demand of Paint. Service Colour. Visited 1 & 2 Sections 38 Div Dismd. Coll. & inspected ammunition in wagons & limbers. Found ammunition in some quite unprotected from weather. & Salvage lying about the lines. Reported same to Staff Capt. R.A.	
	13.		Received 1 1/2 Sub. gun for B/121. Visited Gr.Dn. Stores and Transport lines of 19th (Pioneer) Battn. Welsh Regt. Attended distribution of Brit. stores at all re-filling points. Visited Salvage Group.	V
	14		At Rail head & Gun Park No 3. also to D.D. Corps H.Q. for orders. Called to see A.D.O.S. Corps # at NAOURS.	
	15		Attended meeting at O.Z.A. Ammunition Railhead (PUCHEVILLERS). D.D.O.S Third Army, with the I.O.O. was present also A.D.O.S. V Corps & all D.A.D.O.S. Subject. Care & sorting of Ammunition at	

Army Form C. 2118.

WAR DIARY
INTELLIGENCE SUMMARY
(Erase heading not required.)

D.A.D.O.S 38th Div

July 1918

Place	Date	Hour	Summary of Events and Information	Remarks and references to Appendices
TOUTENCOURT	15		A.R.Ps and method of collecting & packing returned empties etc. Inspected the latter at O.Z.A and also inspected one of the A.R.Ps of the V Corps.	
	16.		Received one 18Pdr gun for A/121 Bde R.F.A. Two water carts and one Wagon P.S. – G.S., all complete harness, arrived for 2nd G. Battalion, being their additional establishment. Visited DaDOS 21 Div. reference coming relief of Division, also 9 OM, and 19/46 Dm W (Lepin).	
	17.		Visited A.R.P. and inspected some H/S shells which had been received wrongly marked as to driving bands & others packed in wrongly marked boxes. Saw Staff Captain R.A. who reported on same. Saw O.C. Signals re/ indents from his Artillery Sub. Sections. Visited Div. Salvage Dump. Attended Railhead. Visited Battery positions of D/121 & D/122 and saw D.C. reference re-	
	18.		return of H/S cartridges in a bitter condition to A.R.P. Lt. Col. A. WATSON A.D.C. admitted to Hospital. Saw 2 M/S guns. Visited (Remainder)	
	19.		Visited 3rd Workshops. Reference delayed repair of vehicles & the return of M/S guns. Visited Corps Salvage Dump & drew some wheels (from M/S vehicle) urgently required by one of the Battalion	
	20.		Received 12 lean runs for same - 4 each - to the Field Coys R.E. Visited A.R.P., Div Reception Camp 115 Inf Brigade HQ and 13/ Field Ambulance. Demanded 2 151Pdr guns to replace worn	
	21.		out No.1 here - one from of pieces. Attended distribution of stores at re fitting grounds. Called in 9OM reference the height of 4.5 How. & carriage destroyed by firematine. D Batt. 121/ 152c. Wired an inclust for replacement of same. Visited HQ Div Train and D.A.C.	

Army Form C. 2118.

D.A.D.O.S.
38th Div.

WAR DIARY
INTELLIGENCE SUMMARY.
(Erase heading not required.)

Instructions regarding War Diaries and Intelligence Summaries are contained in F. S. Regs., Part II. and the Staff Manual respectively. Title pages will be prepared in manuscript.

Place	Date	Hour	Summary of Events and Information	Remarks and references to Appendices
TOUTENCOURT	July 1918			
	22		Visited Transport lines & Wagon lines & Div Stores of A, C, & D batteries 122 Bde R.F.A. & inspected Ammunition in the Wagons. Found four rounds Shrapnel with pushed charge mixed with H.E. in a wagon of C Battery. Reported the circumstances to H.Q. 38 Div R.A.	
	23		Went with Div T.M. Officer to Heavy Mobile Workshop Ra 3 at AUXI LE CHATEAU to see Portable beds for 6" T.M.s being made there. Visited A.R.P. ref the rounds of 18 Pdr found yesterday, & to see the A.O.C. personnel. The sorting of ammunition & the packing & return of Empties was very satisfactory. Visited all the Divl Salvage Dumps, also Q.O.M. 19/46 Divl Workshop (L). Received 16 Lewis Guns for Mine Zeach to R7cr Batteries completing them to 4 per Battery.	
	24		Inspected Ammunition at 1 Sec. D.A.C. also the vehicles reference very heavy demands for Service Colour Paint, & leather fittings etc. Found demands were not justified & informed OC that they must be amended. Inspected Q.O.M. stores & system of recovery of unserviceable gun parts from Batteries. Visited Div Bomb Store + 3 Sec DAC, also Salvage Dump & passed salved Amm's itted as fit for transport to new Corps Dump at PUCHEVILLERS.	
	25			
	26			
	27		Visited A.R.P. prior to it being handed over to 17th Division, whom Artillery relieved the 38 Divl Arty to day. Called at Corps Salvage Dump for stores, also Q.O.M. 19/46 DMWks(L). Capt OWEN returned for duty today, after protectionary course at Ordnance Base depôt HAVRE.	

2353 Wt. W2514/143 700,000 5/15 D.D.&L. A.D.S.S./Forms/C. 2118.

Army Form C. 2118.

WAR DIARY
or
INTELLIGENCE SUMMARY.
(Erase heading not required.)

Instructions regarding War Diaries and Intelligence Summaries are contained in F. S. Regs., Part II. and the Staff Manual respectively. Title pages will be prepared in manuscript.

Place	Date	Hour	Summary of Events and Information	Remarks and references to Appendices
TOUTENCOURT	July 28		Very heavy consignment of stores at Rail head today from HAVRE, now having been received from that Base for six days. Only pack mules made at rapping points in consequence. Visited Salvage Dump, also O.C. 13th Weld Rgt., & inspected Q: M: stores & Battalion workshops.	
	29		Lt. Cmdr D.G/MAC. left for probationary course with C.O.O. HAVRE. (In connection as A.C.O.) Visited N.B. 121 Bde R.F.A. and also wagon lines of A & D Batteries. Inspected the ammunition in limbers & wagons, also the Quartermasters stores. Seemed remainder of stores received yesterday & also clothing etc. received from ROUEN today.	
	30		Visited 38 M.G. Battalion, were transport and stores of three companies out at rest. All the guns of this unit were overhauled in Div. Armourers Shop during past 8 days. Called at 2074 C.M.W (Mov) for some telescopes & binoculars repaired there.	
	31		Received 18 Pdr gun for c/122. Inspected Q.M. stores of 14th & 16th R.W.F. and the Battalion workshops. MK VIII[?] of Field Coy's R.E. Sections of D.A.C. and batteries of 121 Brigade R.F.A were overhauled in Divisional Armr Shop during the month.	

31/7/18

N. Clifford Major.
D.A.D.O.S. 38th Div.

Army Form C. 2118.

WAR DIARY
or
INTELLIGENCE SUMMARY.
(Erase heading not required.)

D.A.D.O.S. 38th Division

Aug. 1918

Vol 33

Place	Date	Hour	Summary of Events and Information	Remarks and references to Appendices
TOUTENCOURT	1918 Aug 1		Received 3000 Blankets for special issue at rate of 1 per man to Div Artillery, Div Train, Signals & all Category "B" men. Visited Salvage Dumps & D.A.D.O.S. 22nd Division for stores. Drew H.S. Carriage from Gun Park for D/121. R.F.A.	
	2.		Visited wagon lines of B/122, C/121 & B/121 & inspected Gun Stores & ammunition in limbers &c.	
	3.		Air Raid last night & attended issue of stores at refilling points. Visited 123 Field Coy R.E. & Salvage Dump.	
	4.		Received one 4.5 How: for D/122. R.F.A. Visited D.A.D.O.S. 17th Division reference stores to be handed over on coming relief.	
	5.		Rail head changed to BERNAVILLE. Division started relieving 17th Div in the line. No change in location of Div HQ or Ordnance Dump. Visited A.D.O.S. V Corps at NAOURS.	
	6.		Inspected Gun Stores at Div HQ, and Nos 3 Coy Div Train. Visited Salvage Dump. Relief of 17th Div Artillery by 38th Artillery started. Ammn Refilling Point at V.S.A. 4.3 (Sheet 57 D) taken over.	
	7.		Railhead changed to CANDAS. D.D.O.S. Third Army inspected Dump & workshops with A.D.O.S. V Corps. Suggested to D.D.O.S. that, owing to difficulty of procuring small stores for use of reinforcing drafts, stocks of same should be kept at Gun Parks for issue under special contracts when required, & local purchase prohibited. Visited A.R.P. & found large accumulations of empties left by outgoing Division, also that the sorting of the ammunition was very imperfectly done.	
	8.		Visited Reserve Camp & inspected R.Q.Rs Stores. Found some serviceable clothing which had been prematurely condemned & showed same to A.A & Q.M.G. who was also at the Camp. Visited 129 Field Amb: & H.Q. 115 Inf Brigade.	

2353 Wt. W3541/B54 700,000 5/15 D. D. & L. A.D.S.S./Forms/C. 2118.

Army Form C. 2118.

WAR DIARY
INTELLIGENCE SUMMARY.
(Erase heading not required.)

D.A.D.O.S.
38th Division
Aug. 1918.

Instructions regarding War Diaries and Intelligence Summaries are contained in F. S. Regs., Part II. and the Staff Manual respectively. Title pages will be prepared in manuscript.

Place	Date	Hour	Summary of Events and Information	Remarks and references to Appendices
TOUTENCOURT	9.		Received heavy consignment of stores from HAVRE including full demand of Service Colour Paint - 3000 lbs of which has been received for past 3 months. Visited Divl. Salvage Dumps & also those of 17th Division just taken over. Visited Transport lines of 3 & 4 Coys 38 Divn Train & inspected Q.M.S. Stores, saddlers & farriers shops etc. Inspected A.R.P. & found all in very good order.	
	10.		Rail head changed to ROSEL. On truck from ROUEN cleared & stores moved at re-filling points. Visited 114 Bde HQ. also wagon lines of B/122 & C/122. & inspected Q.M.Ps Stores & the ammunition in limbers. Drew five salved Lewis guns from Salvage Dump for re-assembly (where possible) in Armrs Shop. Visited Staff Capt RA reference overhaul of Lewis Guns of Batteries, & the issue of Divl Stores at certain change.	
	11			
	12		Inspected Q.M.S stores of 13th & 16th R.W.F. & the Baster Workshops. Inspected Ammunition in limbers at Wagon lines of A/122. & also Q.M.S Stores & saw the O.C. reference very heavy demands for clothing.	
	13.		Visited Salvage Dumps & A.R.Ps. including the ground dump at V.3.d. where salved ammunition fuses (Sheet 57 D) vacated gun positions in Divl area is being collected & re-sorted. Inspected stocks of clothing at Divl Baths.	
	14.		2.O Battery visitors from 38 Div Arty & one from 7 Corps H.A. came in to Divl Armourers Shop for a four days course in repairs to Lewis Guns. Visited IIIth Bde HQ ref. demands for A.A Sights, & special sites for training.	
	15		At Rail head with all lorries, the 8 tons stores returned from HAVRE did not arrive. Visited clean clothing store and examined 1100 pairs of clean socks there which had been picked out as unserviceable mainly thro' abnormal shrinkage at ABBEVILLE laundry. Reported same to A.D.O.S. on his visit today.	

Army Form C. 2118.

WAR DIARY
INTELLIGENCE SUMMARY.
(Erase heading not required.)

D.A.D.O.S.
38th Divn.

Aug. 1918.

Place	Date	Hour	Summary of Events and Information	Remarks and references to Appendices
TOUTENCOURT.	16		Attended issues of stores at re-filling points. Visited Transport lines of 13th Welsh Regt. & inspected R2 Mt's. stores and Battn. Workshops; also those of 19th Welsh Regt. (Reserve). Visited Salvage Dump.	
	17		Truck of stores arrived from ROUEN failed to arrive at Railhead today. Visited H.Q. 115 Brigade (Aug) and inspected with Staff Captain, his forward dumps of S.D. Clothing & underclothing for exchange when men are gassed, & also the system of accounting. Inspected A.R.P. and the Div's Ammunition (Reserve) Store.	
	18.		Cleared trucks of Stores (ROUEN) today. One due from HAYRE failed to arrive. Received one Field + Carriage for A/121 Bde. no place shall fire. Called on D.C. 14th Welsh Regt. ref excessive demand for S.D. Clothing, which he reduced by 2/3. Received some wilfully mutilated S.D. Clo. from 10th S.W.B., Reported same to Bde H.Q, & took it up for inspection, & the state circumstances. Visited Div. Salvage Dump.	
	19.		One truck at Railhead today. The one due yesterday still not arrived. Visited H.Q. Div. Train Coy. reference excessive demands for accessories. Visited also Gun Parks nos 3, ref. gun unned yesterday, also Divisional Reception Camp, 129 Field Ambulance & 130 Field Ambulance. A.D.O.S. V Corps called in afternoon.	
	20.		The truck from HAYRE due on 18th arrived today, & stores issued at re filling points. Visited Transport lines of 15th Welsh, 14th & 16th R.W.F. & inspected Bn Mr Stores & Battalion Workshops. Visited also Salvage Dump. Sub.Corpl D.G.MAY A.O.C. returned to duty from Instructional course at Corp, HAYRE. Pro stores at Rail head today. The four lorries were detailed by S.M.T.O. for R.E. work in connection with the operations starting today. Obtained special sanction for one lorry in afternoon to fetch 18 Pdr Gun from Gun Park for B/121 R.F.A. Visited 114 & 115 H.Qrs and Div. A.R.P.	
	21.			

A.D.S.S./Form C. 2118.

Army Form C. 2118.

WAR DIARY
INTELLIGENCE SUMMARY.
(Erase heading not required.)

D.A.D.O.S
38 Div
Aug 18

Place	Date	Hour	Summary of Events and Information	Remarks and references to Appendices
TOUTENCOURT	22		Railhead changed to BELLE EGLISE. Cleared two trucks of rations. Issues were to units severe but rations were insufficiently warm clothing dry batteries. Visited H.Q. 115 Inf Bde reference the return of unserviceable worn clothing dry batteries.	Sheet 57 D.
	23		One truck of articles cleared today. Visited Transport lines of D Coy 38 Batt R.S.C. reference vehicles & harness destroyed by enemy bomb & inspected R&M stores. Visited 38 Div M.T Coy Head quarters & inspected Quartermasters system of accounting etc & units dirt repair shop.	
	24		Visited Divisional Artillery & found their Divisional Ordnance staff of 1 W.O. & 2 Pte A.O.C. with one lorry reported for duty. 38 Div. H.Q. moved to HEDAUVILLE.	V.4.d. cent.
HEDAUVILLE	25		Moved Ordnance Office & Dump to HEDAUVILLE. Visited new Salvage Dump, also O.O. V Corps Dumps at HAO1RS for shoes, also A.D.O.S. Div HQ. moved to USNA REDOUBT.	P 34.a.7.2. W.2.a.b.
	26		No stores from Base. Visited Staff Captains of Infantry Brigades, & Salvage Dumps. One truck stores from HAVRE cleared today. Only stores urgently needed were issued reparations held till troops come out of line. Visited Staff Capt R.A. reference collection of 3.18 Pdr anti tank guns left in Lestartains. Visited also Div Pole Transport lines and Salvage Dump.	
	28		Visited Staff Captains of three Inf Brigades at the rear HQ. And obtained information as to requirements to replace losses in ordnance forms & equipment. Collected certain stores from Salvage Dump	

Required for N. W. (signature)

2353 Wt. W2544/1454 700,000 5/15 L, D. & L.   A.D.S.S./Form/C.2118.

Army Form C. 2118.

WAR DIARY
INTELLIGENCE SUMMARY.
(Erase heading not required.)

D.A.D.O.S.
38th Division

Aug. 1918

Place	Date	Hour	Summary of Events and Information	Remarks and references to Appendices
LA BOISSELLE	Aug 29		Moved Ordnance Office and Dump to LA BOISELLE. All under canvas. Received one truck of stores from PAYRE which was dumped at new position. Sheet 57 D. X.14.6.6.0.	Sheet 57 D. X.14.6.6.0.
	30		Clewed up & captured M.G.s to Railhead for previous day. Truck of clothing due today did not arrive. Posted 122 Bde R.F.A., H.Q. D.A.C., 38 M.G. Batt'n, and Staff Capt 112 Bde. Clewed 2 Captured German Field Guns (Anti-tank) and 20 M.Gs to Railhead.	
	31		Demanded 2. 4.5 Hows and 2. 18 Pdr Guns to replace 4 g/s tooth at Railhead. Visited Salvage Dump & collected large number of Lewis Gun Magazines & free Lewis pans and various equipment for re-issue. Demanded 4 Lewis Guns to replace lost, and re-issued six from Brit. Slsh after repair.	

M C Murray
D.A.D.O.S. 38 Dn

Army Form C. 2118.

WAR DIARY
INTELLIGENCE SUMMARY.
(Erase heading not required.)

D.A.D.O.S. 38th (Welsh) Divn

Sept. 1918

Place	Date	Hour	Summary of Events and Information	Remarks and references to Appendices
LA BOISSELLE	Sept 1		Rail-head moved to AVELUY. Supply train ordered for 3 pm did not arrive till 9 pm & then found that Ordnance truck had been detached. Visited 113 Bde H.Q. Salvage Dumps & A.R.P. Demanded 4 Lewis Guns for 113 Bde to replace lost. Received 1 B.Per for 20/310. "Inaccuracy".	Sheet 57 D X.14. & 6.0.
	2.		Visited advanced Divn HQ at S.9.6.9.9. (Sheet 57 c) & saw Staff Capt R.A. reference possible requirements. Wired an indent to Base for 30 hot food containers for use of Infantry. Collected large quantity of salved Lewis gun equipment & other stores for re-issue from Salvage Dump. Demanded 6 Lewis Guns to replace others lost by 15th Welsh Regt.	
	3.		Advanced Divn HQ moved to LES BOEUFS, near Divn HQ moved to S.9.6.9.9. Visited A.D.O.S. V Corps at SENLIS. also the 3. Staff Captains of Inf. Brigades to ascertain requirements.	Sheet 57 e. T.4.O.4.5.
	4		Cleared one truck of Clothing from ROUEN – Special demand for Pending re equipment when Divn comes out of the line. Visited transport-lines of 113 & 114 Inf Bdes & Salvage Dump.	
LES BOEUFS	5		Rear Divn HQ joined Advanced Divn HQ at LES BOEUFS. Ordnance Officer and Stenop moved to LES BOEUFS. Cleared one truck of stores at new Rail-head at BEAUVENCOURT.	* T.O.L.
	6		Relief of Division completed today. Made heavy issues of clothing to Infantry & M.G. Battalion. Cleared two trucks of articles from MIRAUMONT rail-head, as no facilities for off loading these trail at BEAUVENCOURT.	
	7		Demanded 48 Lewis Guns for 115 Brigade to replace lost. Sent a lorry to Gun Park to fetch these and also the large number of Magazines L.G. required. Gun Park was only able to issue 20 guns.	

Army Form C. 2118.

WAR DIARY
or
INTELLIGENCE SUMMARY.
(Erase heading not required.)

D.A.D.O.S. 38th (Welsh) Div
Sept 1918

Place	Date	Hour	Summary of Events and Information	Remarks and references to Appendices
	Sept.			
LES BOEUFS	8		Visited Staff Captains 114 & 115 Bde. Inf. re-equipping; also Staff Capt. R.A. re the loss of an 18Pr. gun & carriage. This latter was overturned in a shell hole & presumably cabled by another Division. Information re a battery gun Pit. sight returned to battery senior Rt	(Forgot no 10.5)
	9		Visited Salvage Dump & obtained large number of items from Suspense & equipment for re issue. Divisional Artillery of 62nd Div'n reported their formation. Ordnance Personnel were transferred also today. Two loads of stores recd from HAVRE & ROUEN clrd from BEAULENCOURT.	
	10		Visited Adv. Gun Park for stores, also 38 M.G. Batt's and transport lines of 113th Welsh Rgt. Cleared 2 lorries of vehicles from Railhead. Visited Staff Capt. 113 (Inf) Bde. re. re-equipping	
	11		The Division relieved 17th Div'n in the line. Div. HQ. moved to ETRICOURT. Visited A.D.O.S. V Corps at SENLIS. ref obtaining wire cutters urgently required. Visited also G.O.R. & Corps. Ordnance Office & Dumps moved to ROCQUIGNY. Cleared 1 lorrie stores from Railhead, also a	O.22.d.7.0. Sheet 57c.
ROCQUIGNY	12.		lot of salvaged stores for re issue. Received one 18Pr. for D/122 and 4.5 Hyn. Ammn. for D/122.	
	13		Demanded the Lewis guns complete for 14 Welsh to replace lost; also an 18Pr. for G/121.	
	14		Visited Staff Captains R.A., 113 (Inf) Bde & 115 (Inf) Bde, also Ammns Refilling point. Inspected WD Clothing and underclothing held at Gas Changing Centre also Div. Bomb store.	
	15		Visited 13 Welsh Rgt. transport lines ref. articles of equipment required. Lorry from Gun Park A.S. not call. Sent a lorry there for articles of gun, 1,000 Magazines L.G., also 58 bags of [illegible] were filled are overdue for issue.	

2353 Wt. W2544/1454 700,000 5/15 L.D. & L. A.D.S.S./Forms/C. 2118.

Army Form C. 2118.

WAR DIARY
INTELLIGENCE SUMMARY.
(Erase heading not required.)

D.A.D.O.S. 38th Div.

Sept 1916.

Place	Date	Hour	Summary of Events and Information	Remarks and references to Appendices
ROCQUIGNY.	16		Received one 4.5 How. & Carriage for D/122 to replace one destroyed by "Prematire". Visited Staff Captains of 113 & 114 Inf Brigades, also Salvage Dump.	Sheet 57c. O.22. d.7.0.
	17		One truck of stores from HAVRE. 115.1st Divisional Signal Coy due by this Kinde and urgently required did not arrive. Wired a "hastener" for same to Base. Visited Gun Park ref. non-receipt of Lewis Gun Magazines, over 1300 due & none available. T/Sub Cond A. WATSON, A.O.C. reported for duty on re-posting after evacuation to Base, sick. Rear Divisional H.Q. moved to O.36.c. (Sheet 57c.) at 6 p.m.	
	18		Demanded one 18 Pdr gun and two 18th Carriages condemned for wearing & bore repair. Collected 450 Magazines L.G. from Salvage Dumps for repair or re-issue. Visited Transport lines of 114th & 115th Weld Regts. also Staff Capt 114th Inf Bde. Received 5 Lewis Guns for 13/12 R.W.F.	
	19.		Visited Staff Capt. R.A. Relief of Division in line by 17th Division commenced. San. Sec. D.A.D.O.S. 17th Div. ref. handing over of stores. Received one Vickers Gun to replace one destroyed.	
	20.		Mail head changed to ROCQUIGNY. Demanded (by wire, 19th) blankets to complete Division to one per man. Went to Gun Park for urgently required stores. Visited 123 Field Coy. ref Transport repairs. Demanded one 3" Stokes Mortar complete for 114th T.M.B. to replace destroyed by shell fire.	
	21		Received 950 Magazines L.G. from Gun Park. Demanded 26 Lewis Guns & 3 Vickers Guns to replace lost. Visited 38th D.C. Battn. & 114th Bde. H.Q. to hasten "re-fitting" material. Visited Reception Camp and	

Army Form C. 2118.

D.A.D.O.S.
38th (Welsh) Division
Sept 1918

WAR DIARY
INTELLIGENCE SUMMARY
(Erase heading not required.)

Place	Date	Hour	Summary of Events and Information	Remarks and references to Appendices
ROCQUIGNY.	Sep/r 21.		Inspected Quarter-master stores.	Sheet 57c
	22.		Heavy consignment of stores received from HAVRE, including 1" Pistols Signal very recently received. Visited Salvage Dumps — Div'l & Corps —; also 115 Brigade reference indents for re-equipping.	Dress'd F.O.
	23.		Sent two lorries to Gun Park & brought away 37 Lewis Guns, Hotchkiss Guns & large quantity of magazines & spare parts due to complete deficiencies in recent actions. Blankets demanded on 19th admired as due at Railhead today, but failed to arrive. Visited Staff Captains of 113 Inf Bde and 115 Inf Brigade, also 1st & 16th Battns R.W.F. reference re-equipping.	
	24.		Blankets still overdue. Telegraphic enquiries to regulating station to ensure arrival tomorrow. Visited Staff Capt 114 Inf Brigade and Staff Capt R.A., also D.O.M. & Salvage Dumps.	
	25.		Received and issued 5000 Blankets completing issue of 1 per man. Visited transport lines of 123, 124 & 151 Field Coys and inspected 6/R.W. Stores & transport vehicles.	
	26.		Drew 9000 Jerkins from D.O. I Corps, as part of winter issue, & moved all, giving preference to fighting troops. Demanded a further 2000 from Base to complete all demands. Received one 18Pdr. gun & carriage for Q/122. reference scoring & "base repair" respectively.	
	27.		Completed issue of the 64 Lewis Guns of the M.G. Batt'n in Div'l Armourers Shop. A.D.O.S. I Corps called. Received warning order of move forward of Division tomorrow, and arranged with Q to receive back the blankets recently issued, for storage in a Sup Dump til Gain required.	

2353 Wt. W2544/1-54 700,000 5/15 D.D.&L. A.D.S.S./Forms/C. 1118.

Army Form C. 2118.

D.A.D.O.S.
38th (Welsh) Division
Sept 1916

WAR DIARY
INTELLIGENCE SUMMARY.
(Erase heading not required.)

Instructions regarding War Diaries and Intelligence Summaries are contained in F. S. Regs., Part II. and the Staff Manual respectively. Title pages will be prepared in manuscript.

Place	Date	Hour	Summary of Events and Information	Remarks and references to Appendices
				Sheet 57c
ROCQUIGNY	28		Divisional H.Q. (advanced) moved to V.18.c.1.9., near H.Q., with Ordnance removed in present O.22.d.7.0. location. Received all blankets from Infantry, M.G. Battn, & R.E. Field Coys and placed them in Dump at O.23.d.5.0. Visited Staff Capt. 115 Bde, & H.Q. & 2nd Sect. 38 D.A.C. Procured from Railhead an X.T. fork pole for 16 R.W.F. to enable vehicle to be moved with Battn.	
	29		Visited 9.0.M. reference repairs to Vehicles & disposal of Lumber Wagons. 157th returned in exchange of carriage limber. Visited Staff Captains R.A., & 114 Inf Brigade.	
	30		Railhead changed to F/N5. Cleared 1 truck of stores including the remainder of blankets to complete to 1 per man, & delivered all stores to units at their transport lines.	

M.O.W.M. Major
D.A.D.O.S. 38th Divn

Army Form C. 2118.

WAR DIARY
or
INTELLIGENCE SUMMARY.

(Erase heading not required.)

D.A.D.O.S. 38th (Welsh) Division.

Oct. 1918

Place	Date 1918 Oct.	Hour	Summary of Events and Information	Remarks and references to Appendices
ROCQUIGNY.	1		War Diarial HQ joined D Div. HQ at V.18.c.1.9. (SOREL). Re-issued all blankets to infantry units. Moved Div Armourers Shop & Bopi-shop to SOREL preparatory to move of Ordnance HQ store tomorrow.	Sheet 57c 0.22.d.7.0.
NURLU	2		Advance office & dump, together with Arm's Shop &c moved to NURLU.	V.23.d.7.2
	3		Closed Div.g general stores (from HAVRE) & one truck of Vehicles from Railhead – FINS. Visited Staff Capt. R.A. and Staff Capt 114 Bde. Overhauled 12 Hotchkiss Guns of 9th Welsh & 302 Sqdn.	Sheet 62c F.1.d.7.0.
	4		Advanced Div. HQ moved to EPEHY. Visited Inf.B. Batts., 15 Welsh Regt & 16 Welsh.	
	5		Received one 18 Pdr. Gun for A/121 Bde to replace scoring. Completed issue of Jerkins to all units in receipt of 2000 today from ROUEN.	
	6		Visited A.D.O.S. I Corps reference reinforcements required to complete staff. Orders being received to send 6 w.o. to base. Visited 38 In.G. Batty. and 15 Welsh Regt. ref. Transport Equipment.	
EPEHY	7		General Ordnance HQ to EPEHY. Closed one truck general stores from Railhead (FINS).	
	8		Visited Staff Captain of 113 & 114 (Inf.) Brigades. Closed two trucks from Railhead, one of which had been overdue some days.	
	9		089/88 A/Cont. F.R.OWEN – chief clerk – and 07189 Act-Cpl D.G.MAY left for base, on being posted to C.B.O. HAVRE to take up commission as A.C.o.O. Received large consignment of general stores from HAVRE which could not be issued owing to all units being on the move.	

WAR DIARY or INTELLIGENCE SUMMARY

Army Form C. 2118.

D.A.D.O.S. 38th Divn.
Feb 1918

Place	Date	Hour	Summary of Events and Information	Remarks and references to Appendices
VILLERS OUTRÉAUX	10		Moved Ordnance H.Q.s to VILLERS OUTRÉAUX, to which place Div. H.Q. is located from today. Left Div. Mun.y Shop for removal tomorrow. Cleared 1 truck of stores from Rail head, 57.K.S.	Sheet 57 b. T. 15 & 58.
	11		Div. MS. moved to CLARY. Received 9 Lewis & 2 Vickers guns for 16 R.W.F. & 38 M.G. Battalion respectively. Cleared one truck General stores from Rail head & moved Div. Armrs. Shop & Boot shop. Unable to issue any stores to units as two lorries were detailed by Q. for other purposes, and all units were too far in advance to send transports.	
	12		Div. HQ. moved to BERTRY. Ordnance Dump unable to move owing to congestion of stores. All lorries were sent out to units with stores for same, and all "returned" Ordnance cleared to R.H. Demanded one 18 Pdr for B/121 for shrapnel scoring, also 13 Lewis Guns for 15 Welch R. & 1 & 3 Siege M.M.	
BERTRY	13		Moved Ordnance H.Q.s — office & own stores — to the Barracks at BERTRY. Cleared one truck P.&.d.1.6 (13 ton) General stores from Rail head to new dump. Collected 20 Lewis Guns & over 400 Strops ..... from Salvage dump for overhaul & re-issue. Average time for lorries to go to Rail head is now about 3½ hours each way, owing to great distance and so much traffic on roads.	
	14		Cleared truck of clothing, including 16,000 winter vests from Railhead, and completed move of stores and Armourers Shop to new dump. Visited Salvage dump & collected 5 Lewis guns.	
	15		Rail head changed to MASNIERES. Visited 113 Bde Staff Capt. re: re-equipping of Battalions. Issued Winter vests to units of Brigades.	
	16		Cleared 1 truck stores from Rail head.	

Army Form C. 2118.

WAR DIARY
or
INTELLIGENCE SUMMARY.
(Erase heading not required.)

D.A.D.O.S. 38th Division

Oct 1918

Place	Date	Hour	Summary of Events and Information	Remarks and references to Appendices
BERTRY.	17		Cleared 1 Truck General Stores from FINS Railhead. Lorries all went to MASNIERES and found in arrival there that owing to an accident train was diverted to FINS.	
	18		Visited Staff Captains of 113 and 115 Inf Bdes, also S.O.M. 19/46 O.M.W.(L) Reference receipts of Ammn Wagons from Gun Park for the Division, & return of vehicles.	
	19		Demanded one 18 Pdr Wagon Amm'n for B/121 replace condemned. Received one 3" Stokes T.M for 113 T.M Batty also two 18 Pdr guns for C/122 & B/121 respectively.	
	20		Railhead changed to MARCOING. Sent lorries to clean two trucks of winter clothing due but Supply train failed to arrive. Demanded one 18 Pdr & carriage for C/122 R.F.A. to replace one destroyed by premature.	
	21		Cleared 1 Truck of Ammn woollen from Railhead. Only two lorries available, two being in workshops, & as Division could not supply more transport the second truck of winter clothing was dumped for clearing tomorrow.	
	22		Visited D.D.O.S. Third Army at MASNIERES. ref. re-inforcements due to the Ordnance staff. The Major General commanding visited the Ord. Dump, workshops etc. Cleared remainder of woollen clothing from Rail-head & handed from all to O/c Divl Baths for exchange with units for Cotton ones. Cleared also one Truck) vehicles. Demanded 18 Pdr Sun for C/121 and one for A/121 condemned for wear & tear'ing respectively.	

Army Form C. 2118.

WAR DIARY
of
INTELLIGENCE SUMMARY.
(Erase heading not required.)

D.A.D.O.S.
38th Division.
Oct. 1918

Place	Date	Hour	Summary of Events and Information	Remarks and references to Appendices
	Oct.			
BERTRY	23		Rail head changed to CAUDRY. Sent lorries to clear a truck from HAVRE but they returned empty as Supply train did not arrive. S.B557. Temp. Sub Cond. ROLLAND, O.D., A.O.C. reported for duty as Chief Clerk. Collected large quantity of stores for Salvage Dump.	Sheet 57.b.
"	24		Adv D.O.S. moved to ANATAN. K26.d.7.4 (Sheet 57.b). Cleared 1 truck stores due yesterday.	
"	25		Demanded two 18Pdr Guns for C/122. re-place worn & worn. Rear S.H.Q. moved w/b relieved.	
FOREST	26		Division relieved 33rd Division in line. Whole of Div. HQ moved to RICHEMONT with Exception office and dumps at FOREST. Cleared one truck gun ammunition from Railhead to new position. Drove remainder of Fld Stores under armourer & Bo'sn repair shop to FOREST. Cleared one truck stores from Railhead in afternoon. Supply train again very late in convoy.	K.5.d.6.7 K.12.6.cent.
"	27		Received two 18Pdr guns for C/122, also two Vickers Pistols from 38 A.S. Batt. Visited Staff Capts of three Inf. Brigades, and Salvage Group & arranged removal of salved Lewis guns, magazines & spare parts etc. Gd. Artillery moved to BERTRY for 72 hours rest.	
"	28		Visited Staff Capt. N.A. Defence urgent requirements of batteries and ar. & lorries to collect stores direct to wagon lines. Cleared one truck clothing from Railhead; train again very late.	
"	29		Sent 2 c.m.wts S.D.F. underclothing to advanced Gas'changing centre. Visited Salvage Dump & 30 M.	
"	30		Received two 18Pdrs. Adv.d.29.h. for B/121 & 16/122. re-place worn'. Demanded W.S. Hon't carriage promotion for D/122. Returned 10 repaired vatined Lewis Guns to Sun.Park. Cleared 2 trucks from Rail head.	
"	31			

W.G.Upton Major. D.A.D.O.S. 38 Div.

Army Form C. 2118.

D.A.D.O.S
38th (Welsh) Divn.
Nov 1918

Vol 36

WAR DIARY
or
INTELLIGENCE SUMMARY.
(Erase heading not required.)

Place	Date	Hour	Summary of Events and Information	Remarks and references to Appendices
FOREST	Nov 1st 1918		O/Sgt Smith MAIN.A, A.O.C. joined for duty as Brigade W.O. Demanded one 4.5 How + carriage for D122 to replace "premature", also one 3" Stokes T/M for 115 T.M.Batty.	Sheet 57b. K.12.b.6. cent.
	2		Issued one Finch Gun Sight (HARVE) from CAVDRY Railhead. Collected 11 Lewis Guns + large quantity of salved stores from Salvage Dump for overhaul + re-issue.	
	3		Sent to Gun Park No 3 for special stores for use in operations to-morrow. 2/Lieut. P.S. DRAPER, A.O.D., Chief Army Boot Inspr. joined for special duty, i.e. inspection of Divl + Units' boot-repairing shops. Visited Staff Captain of 113 + 114 Inf. Bdes	
	4		Railhead changed to CAMBRAI owing the bridge outside CAVDRY being mined yesterday. Sent lorries to clear trucks of gun stores which were due yesterday. Truck had been detached + could not be located. Lorries returned empty. Adv.d Div.HQ. moved to ENGLEFONTAINE.	
	5		Sent lorries to CAMBRAI with returned stores + to clear truck already over due + also one truck of vehicles. Neither of these trucks arrived. Rear of New Div HQ moved to LOCQUIGNOL. Q ordered two full lorries to dept moved DHQ. I was therefore unable to issue any stores or collect overhead guns + a truck required for RE issue.	
	6		Railhead changed to CAVDRY. Ordnance Truck had been detached at CAMBRAI so lorries were sent there + the truck cleared. Moved Ord. office + dumps, less Armourer's Workshops, to ENGLEFONTAINE.	Sheet 57A. A.1.b.4.10

ENGLEFONTAINE

Army Form C. 2118.

D.A.D.O.S.
38th (Welsh) Division
Nov. 1918

WAR DIARY
or
INTELLIGENCE SUMMARY.
(Erase heading not required.)

Instructions regarding War Diaries and Intelligence Summaries are contained in F. S. Regs., Part II. and the Staff Manual respectively. Title pages will be prepared in manuscript.

Place	Date	Hour	Summary of Events and Information	Remarks and references to Appendices
	Nov.			
ENGLEFONTAINE	7		One truck from HAVRE advanced. Sent lorries to Railhead to clear it but it had been detached & had not arrived. Wrote Bert. 2/offs to 113 Bde. with Lieut. DRAPER; also our Salvage Group.	Sheet 57a. A.I.K.4.10
LOCQUIGNOL	8		From Rly. LOCQUIGNOL. Sent lorries to Railhead but as no stores had arrived, they picked up the Divisional & Bde. dumps from FOREST & all necessary stores & kept it all on lorries.	Map Ye 1/40,000 1/200,000
	9		On truck from HAVRE arrived 5 day. Wrote Staff Capt. R.A. & Artillery Bde. HQs 113/15. Received One 4.5 How. carriage for 2/112. & other howitzer, also one wagon armt. & 18 Pdr for 6/122.	
	10		Trains from now finding very slow. Very few wires made, as roads are too far away to send in a 3 ton lorry. Saw roads & distances Corps Railhead to CAUDRY.	
	11		Armistice with Germany declared at 11.00 hours. No trucks at Railhead Forest. Sent all forward lorries to Special Rly Point at BERLAIMONT & made issues to all units.	
	12		Lieut. DRAPER, A.D.D. left for duty with XVII Corps. Wrote Salvage Group & instructed about the issue of R.E. stores & clearing R.E. stores & dumps to AULNOYE. Received £20 lorries from Div. HQ and all lorries made double journeys. Railhead changed to SOLESMES.	
	13		Wrote D.A.D.O.S. HQ = 151 Bde. With SQMS. Wrote large issues to units. Salvage.	
AULNOYE	14		Reached from ROUEN all cars not in the ability from. Returned full trucks load of damned equipment and damaged...	
	15		Received two 15 Pdr. wagons amount & limbers to replace lost in river SAMBRE. Wrote Staff Capt.	
	16		115 Inf. Bde. Advanced Office. regarding the batteries...	

Army Form C. 2118.

WAR DIARY
or
INTELLIGENCE SUMMARY.
(Erase heading not required.)

D.A.D.O.S. 38. Div.
Nov. /18

Place	Date	Hour	Summary of Events and Information	Remarks and references to Appendices
AULNOYE	Nov. 17		No stores at Railhead today. Wired to Bavai hastening despatch of clothing and horse rugs.	Sheet 57 U.29 & 3.3.
	18		Received 15 Rds gun and carriage; replacing condemned for "scoring" & "base repair".	
	19		Clear one truck clothing from SOLESMES. Arranged with Div. H.Q. for the salvage of three 18 Pdr wagons amm: & limbers, and one 4.5 How: wagon amm: & limber; also one G.S wagon from river SAMBRE. Asked A.D.O.S. for instructions as to disposal of stores not required for Division. One 18 Pdr wagon & limber only being required to complete.	
	20		Sent all other artillery vehicles to J.O.M. 9/46 D.M. W.(L) for repair.	
	21		Visited ROUEN to hospitals heather of gunnery, as only small proportion of that due was received on 19/11 and many units hastening. Visited 130 & 131 Field (inters).	
	22		Visited all Inf. Brigade H.Qrs & several Rif. Park stores & Battalions; also H.Q. D.A.C. Reference re-equipping indents.	
	23		Received 18000 blankets. Pleased use for boothional borries to clear from Railhead.	
	24		Issued all above blankets to units completing the Division to 2 per man.	
	25		Visited Railhead & Corps Salvage Dump., also 90.M. reference repair of Armd wagons for 115/122.	
	26		Railhead changed to SALESCHES. No stores arrived.	
	27		Captain H. SMITH., A.O.D. arrived from H.Q. Third Army for instructions in the duties of a D.A.D.O.S. of a Division.	Anton's Third Army C/A50. d. 20/11/18

A.D.S.S./Forms/C. 2118.

WAR DIARY
INTELLIGENCE SUMMARY.
(Erase heading not required.)

Army Form C. 2118.

D.A.D.O.S. 38 Div.
Nov 28/18

Place	Date	Hour	Summary of Events and Information	Remarks and references to Appendices
	Nov.			Sheet-54
AULNOYE	28		Gustavus again at Railhead. Went to ROUEN for leather & boots, both very urgently required, many units practically out of Boot Shop supplies only	V.29.63.3.
	29		J.M.T. Pioneers & A.R.K. (granted leave for this month) The stores again at Maresches, have ceased from Rouen to the effects that leather has not available. Supplies due in from time to time will be made immediately to our Shoemakers. Captain F——— Remarks to Q 44.55 "any finding, are now long overdue. It will be again at Maresches " Ammunition supply of boots held up on account of network being available."	BULLINGHAM Q.S.S.S. 38 Div
	30			[signature] Capt a.s. D/DADOS 38 Div

P.103.

Headquarters
38 Div. "S"

Herewith War Diary for
December 1918.

JS Clifford Major

15/1/19. DADVS
38 Div.

Army Form C. 2118.

WAR DIARY
INTELLIGENCE SUMMARY
(Erase heading not required.)

D.A.D.V.S. 3rd (Brit.) Division

Vol 3 / Sheet 51 / W29 F3.2

Place	Date	Hour	Summary of Events and Information	Remarks and references to Appendices
AULNOYE	Nov 1918 1		No Orders at Maubeuge. Visited 121 B Bty.	
	2		No Orders again at Maubeuge. Asst. Staff Captain 113 Bde. B.V.S. (Lt. Theures) this morning about leather & boots, but unable to do anything as no lorries available. I received from Nivelle to the effect that no leather available to issue as boots. Explained this to the different units enquiring.	
	3		No Orders at Maubeuge. This morning Military Train through Aulnoye S - Truck entrance from Berm, failed to arrive.	
	4		No truck again today. Believed to be coming had a truck had arrived. Second train had arrived during the day.	
	5		Visited Maubeuge. One truck from Rouen - Maintenance Wanting for & 6 tons (delivered eight 29th Oct.) Arrived a.m. Stores for 17th Nov. T. 2nd Nov. T. & 10th S.a. B. All satisfactory. Adviced toff. has the liver not arrived here ere this Nivelle. Made remark to write to	
	6		No Orders at Maubeuge. Visited Nos 1 & 3 Sections R.V.C & Staff Captain 115 Brigade.	
	7		Truck arrived containing 15 tons of stores from Havre -	
	8		Visited Maubeuge worked N.V.S. of re bound leaves etc as soon as trucks arrived a bed	

WAR DIARY or INTELLIGENCE SUMMARY

Army Form C. 2118.

Place	Date	Hour	Summary of Events and Information	Remarks and references to Appendices
AULNOYE	1918 Dec 8th (contd)		Got away to Aulnoye & Raithead on a fruitless journey. No promised lorries were in even as truck arrived.	
	9		Am recd. message that truck had arrived. Cleared truck to Magistrating stores. Horse rugs, fitteting gear, paint. BAZMS asked for a return of those ordered by this evening. Lorry truck numbers taken or wheels. Machine Guns & Trench mortars were sent to the Base.	
	10		Trade issues 2-day ration. Ammunition 80 harm & ammunition on the 9th.	
	11		Visited Baptries 9 iW 13 & 14 held formed Amn. satisfactory. Visits (A.C. K/121 Battery). Truck arrived from Rouen containing 4 tons Clothing. Returned as very lost & unserviceable stores. Visited A/M Store 15th Brigade.	Try ? try to try?
	12		Visited Staff Captain 113th Brigade. Cleared truck containing 9tons of Clothing & 50 to	
	13		Mens issues to various Units. No sufficient Pretoriad to hold dumps to.	
	14			
	15		wired Units to misstanding indents.	
	16		Arrived Rouen to hasten supply of boots after having gone carefully into the matter Gave recd. satisfying to Wadam & Nelson of 2 Weber containing Clothing & Belt Stores &	
	17		Sent off to from Rouen (Stores) Visited AD of XIII Corps. Sent my load of stores from Rouen for Rouen. Batt & N.Es. Got Units taking Bases down to prepare for the advance.	

2353 Wt W2544/454 700,000 5/15 D.D.&L. A.D.S.S./Form/C. 2118.

WAR DIARY or INTELLIGENCE SUMMARY

Army Form C. 2118.

Place	Date	Hour	Summary of Events and Information	Remarks and references to Appendices
AULNOYE	1918 18 Nov		Railhead changed to Le Quesnoy. Visited Staff Capt. 113 Div & 2/M 13 AARch. Division. Made arrangements for trains to go. Visited N°16 BM/GS Light ANDRECHIES	
	19		Rearranged with Regt. to send in 2 carts noon for repairs belonging to B/24 & B/122 Batteries. Two Fords arrived. Also one Austin Ambulance truck + 1 from Havre. B/24 Echelon cleared no hospital or vehicles on Calais truck - Wired for vans & also asked reports that have been made.	
	20		Visited Army H.Qrs. Finch. Visited Asst. Capt. 113 Div. Lorry & enquired after Army Lorry.	
	21		Left Aulnoye to report at B.A.E.D. at 9 a.m. Signed Capt. M.C.C. Rly T.O. L.2 3/12/18.	
	22		Lorry was ever getting to Rouen to fetch bolts which are urgently required. No stores at Railhead Today.	
	23			
	24		One German Mauser Field Gun taken to Railhead LE QUESNOY. Lorry returned from ROUEN with bolts, the majority of which were immediately issued.	
	25		Visited Staff Capt. 11th Div etc.	
	26		Base changed to CALAIS.	

Army Form C. 2118.

WAR DIARY
or
INTELLIGENCE SUMMARY.
(Erase heading not required.)

Instructions regarding War Diaries and Intelligence Summaries are contained in F. S. Regs., Part II. and the Staff Manual respectively. Title pages will be prepared in manuscript.

Place	Date	Hour	Summary of Events and Information	Remarks and references to Appendices
AULNOYE.	27		One truck from HAVRE arrived & re-consigned to CORBIE in view of pending move of Division. Cleared all returned Ord. Stores to Rail head & also one 77 mm. German captured gun and limber.	
	28		12 t. all kalibers. divisional reserve etc. on rail & consigned to CORBIE.	
	29		One returned Brown's wagon & limber cleared to Railhead, LE QUESNOY.	
	30		Ord H.Q. started the move to new area, QUERRIEU. Ambulance Staff still remaining.	
			Adv. left AULNOYE 08.00 hrs & arrived PONT NOYELLES at 16.00 hrs. No accommodation available. Waited awaiting for the night & billeted personnel at Area Commd's Office.	
PONT NOYELLES.	31		Truck sent to Accommodation & Spares Office & Ord. Depots etc. at PONT NOYELLES. Rail head CORBIE. Six others arrived Ist. Ord. H.Q. opened at GLISY.	2/1/1919.

J.W. Clifford Major
D.A.D.O.S. 38th Div.

Army Form C. 2118.

D.A.D.O.S.
38th (Welsh) Div.

WAR DIARY
INTELLIGENCE SUMMARY.
(Erase heading not required.)

Place	Date	Hour	Summary of Events and Information	Remarks and references to Appendices
	1919.			
DOINGT NOYELLES.	1 Jan		One truck of general stores at railhead CORBIE cleared today. Major B. CLIFFORD R.A.O.C. returned from 30 days leave in ENGLAND.	
	2.		One truck clothing & gradery received from CALAIS, no boots received.	
	3.		Welsh Staff Capt. R.A., R.O.O. at CORBIE and I.O.M. 19/45 Div. Workshops (L.)	
	4.		The HARPE train decamped from LE QUESNOY on 27 Dec arrived today. The seals were broken & there were evident traces of tampering with the stores. Contents were checked in presence of representations of R.T.O. & Div. Authorities as well as tracing the Railhead & Base Ordnance. The bicycle three cases manage lost, and four payment parcels containing 2 loaves each, were missing.	
	5.		Inspection of Railhead. Telegraphed an indent for 50 Jerjeen stoves. Visited 13th & 15th Welsh Regt. & inspected Bn Pioneers & battalion workshops.	
	6.		Two trucks of railhead today containing 8000 blankets and 750 bags P.S. all now cleared & part issue of blankets made to units.	
	7.		About one truck general stores from Calais. No boots received & units hastening supply. Wired home to hasten despatch & again referred shortage to A.D.O.S. V Corps.	
	8.		Completed issue of Field blanket. An issue to all units made A.D.O.S. V Corps at VIGNACOURT.	

Army Form C. 2118.

WAR DIARY
or
INTELLIGENCE SUMMARY.
(Erase heading not required.)

Instructions regarding War Diaries and Intelligence Summaries are contained in F. S. Regs., Part II. and the Staff Manual respectively. Title pages will be prepared in manuscript.

Remarks and references to Appendices

Jan 1919.

Place	Date	Hour	Summary of Events and Information
PONT NOYELLES	9.		Cleared one truck stores at railhead from CALAIS. Still no boots arrived. Informed by Third Army that boots were short at Base. Informed DADOS of this, and arranged that all units be instructed to pay very special attention to repairs of boots. Visited Staff Capt. R.A. and O.C. 1st Brigade R.F.A. to explain above & see the condition of boots in the Divl. Artillery.
	10.		Visited 2nd R.W.S. and 17th R.W.S. reference supply of boots & inspected the Batt. shop. The Divl. Boot repair shop put on work entirely for artillery units, men coming in and waiting the while their boots were repaired.
	11.		Visited H.Q. R.E. reference supply of billet furniture for R.A.O.C. detachment. Visited Staff Capt. 1st 124 Brigade (A.F.) Received two water carts for B/121 & D/122 respectively.
	12.		Sent off two lorries to CAMBRAI to fetch 500 pairs Gum boots Thigh from C.O. Third Army Troops No 1 in accordance with instructions from A.D.O.S. of Corps.
	13.		Cleared three trucks of stores from railhead containing wheels, weapon equipment & 504 pairs Gum Boots Thigh. Visited Staff Capt. R.A. and H.Q. Divl. Amm. Column.
	14.		Visited 115 Inf. Brigade to R. reference articles of camp equipment; also 38 H.G. Batty & reported R.H. since yesterday. Informed Gum boots received yesterday to units for issue immediately. Bde H.Q. moved to QUERRIEU.

WAR DIARY or INTELLIGENCE SUMMARY

Army Form C. 2118.

Jan 1919

Place	Date	Hour	Summary of Events and Information	Remarks and references to Appendices
PONT NOYELLES	15		Pro stores from Base Depot. Visited S.O.M. 15/46, D.H.W. reference repairs of T.M. Dump Prys and motor vehicles. Visited wagon lines of batteries of 122 Bde & inspected Q.M. Stores.	
	16		Two trucks general stores & clothing from CALAIS 15hrs. Only 25% of kits demanded were received & a similar proportion of grinding. Drew from Div. 21 Div some grinding which was surplus there. Reported deficiencies to A.D.T. & to Div HQ. General O'Neill	
	17		run down to Battalions to attended "Presentation" ceremonies. Pro stores received at Railhead. Visited 159 & 130 Field Ambulances, also A.D.V.S. Corps.	
	18		Cleared one truck govt. stores, & one truck vehicles from Rail head. ⅔ Capt. E.E. HILLS. R.A.O.C. from GO. Third Army Troops (M.T.) joined for duty. Lt. G.O.C. 38th Division inspected the workshops and stores.	
	19		Pro stores at Railhead. Attended rail head, and D.A.Q. with Capt. Hills.	
	20		Cleared two trucks general stores from rail head. Visited A.D.V.S. Y Corps, also C.R.E. 38th Divn and inspected boot repair shop at R.E. dump.	
	21		Major B CLIFFORD proceeded to Y Corps H.Q. to act as A.D.V.S. temporary during absence on leave of Lt. Col. SPRAYNER.	Putting field and 9/4/59 dated 19/1/19 Maj W B. W B A.D.V.S. 38th Div
	22		Captain E.E. HILLS took over duties of D.A.D.O.S. temporary. W B Clifford Major A.D.V.S. 38th Div	

Army Form C. 2118.

WAR DIARY
or
INTELLIGENCE SUMMARY.
(Erase heading not required.)

Instructions regarding War Diaries and Intelligence Summaries are contained in F. S. Regs., Part II. and the Staff Manual respectively. Title pages will be prepared in manuscript.

Place	Date	Hour	Summary of Events and Information	Remarks and references to Appendices
PONT NOYELLES	22		No Smoke received from Law. Attended A.H.Q.	
	23		Five Smoke received. Smoke Gen Stores - Smoke Mask - Smoke draught poles. Smok. bar Stores badly differed. Few Boots conformed to demands received. Visited A.H.Q. Motor jam in Workshops. imposable road Authent.	
	24		No Smoke received from Laon.	
	25		Visited A.H.Q.	
	26		Visited C.R.E. and Authent.	
	27		One smoke received from Laon. Visited Authent and C.R.E.	
	28		Car in Workshops. Visited A.H.Q.	
	29		Car still in Workshops. Stores taken out by lorries to 113 & 115 & the A.D. All stores demanded by docks. Major Belford R.A.O & A.D.O.S II Corps	
	30		Collected and inspected Rough 1 Workshops.	
	31		Visited Ration Dumps at Daours and for the Road. also Authent. Visited Authent also A. Gardens.	

E. C. Mills. Capt.
for A.D.O.S. 38 Division

WAR DIARY

D.A.D.O.S. 38th (Welsh) Division

Army Form C. 2118.

Feb 1919

Vol 39

INTELLIGENCE SUMMARY

Place	Date	Hour	Summary of Events and Information	Remarks and references to Appendices
Sart Nogelles	1		Visit L.O.F. & Corps H.Q. to interview A.D.O.S	
	2		Visited abo 194th Advance Mobile Workshops.	
	3		One Limber removed from Breakaway Boots & Saddlery Stores & Ordnance Stores ADOS filled at Dielkirk. No stores to be returned to Calais.	
	4			
	5		ADOS called out inspected dumps and workshops.	
	6		One truck received at Dielkirk. Stores taken out by lorries to 113 S/10 Bde (Infantry)	
	7		Visited ADOS. Also visited Dielkirk and arranged for stores to be stored at Dielkirk in the event of Mons Cemeteries coming into force. Visited Dielkirk, also H.Q. 114 Inf Bde (Infantry) & 13 R Welch Regt.	
	8		Dielkirk at Dolmanville	
	9		Visited 194th Ord. Mobile Workshops also Dielkirk. Called on divisional Supplying H.Q. on the subject of drawing preliminarily to leaving for Egypt. Also Witnessed to C.R.A.	
	10			

WAR DIARY or INTELLIGENCE SUMMARY

Army Form C. 2118.

(Erase heading not required.)

Place	Date	Hour	Summary of Events and Information	Remarks and references to Appendices
	May 11		Visited Southend also 1/4th Ordnance Mobile Workshops.	
	12		Visited 2/4th Ord. M. Workshops regarding furniture from Mess Gun Park.	
	13		Southend closed from Rose to Lowestoft. No trucks received from Base.	
	14		Visited I.O.M.Q. also I.O. to H.Q.	
	15		Visited Southend, also Workshops.	
	16		Nothing of importance occurred	
	17		Visited Southend during morning. Visited 16th Infantry Bde H.Q.	
	18		During morning visited Southend. Afternoon visited Infe H.Q.	
	19		Visited Southend regarding I.C.S. Lieut Col Granger A.D.O.S. ? office.	
	20		Visited Southend - arranged for despatch of one truck stores to Paris.	
	21		Nothing of importance to record	
	22		Nothing to record	
	23		Consultation at Southend with A.D.O.S. office Major Stephens regarding I.C.S. to be established at Portsmouth.	
	24		Re issue of General stores received at Southend.	

Army Form C. 2118.

WAR DIARY
or
INTELLIGENCE SUMMARY.
(Erase heading not required.)

Instructions regarding War Diaries and Intelligence Summaries are contained in F. S. Regs., Part II. and the Staff Manual respectively. Title pages will be prepared in manuscript.

Feby 1919.

Place	Date	Hour	Summary of Events and Information	Remarks, and references to Appendices
PONT NOYELLES	25		Visited Rainneville. D.A.D.O.S. 19/46 Div. Met Notadolph to arrange inspection of Dheles to consumation.	
	26		Visited Railhead. Received orders from ADOS to proceed to Vauchelles to open LOS	
	27		Attended I Corps to conference regarding freeing and working of LOS Major & Clifford M.C. returned to duty from I Corps. E Littlehoft RAVC	
	28		Forty-seven units - mainly Heavy Artillery - transferred to this Division for Ordnance Services from 2D vCorps Corps. One truck of personal stores at Railhead arrived with seals intact, but contents had been tilfered.	

JCM Mortimer
D.A.D.O.S. 38 Div.

WAR DIARY or INTELLIGENCE SUMMARY

Army Form C. 2118.

D.A.D.O.S. 38th (Welsh) Divn.

March 1919

Place	Date	Hour	Summary of Events and Information	Remarks and references to Appendices
PONT NOYELLES	1		Went to POULAINVILLE to arrange moving in 38 defended stores with a few received more finer general stores which was also dumpt.	
	3		Captain E.E. HILLS, R.A.O.C. left for duty with 52nd Division.	2nd Lt. Rutherford A9/19904 at 24/2/19
POULAINVILLE	4		Moved Office & dump to POULAINVILLE and opened Sub Coll. Station. Returned stores by lorries to units of 113 Bde. & 38 Div Artillery. Visited A.D.O.S. & Corps at Thyencourt.	
	5		[illegible]	
			[illegible] R.A.M.C. [illegible]	
	6		Replied [illegible]	
	7		[illegible]	
	8		[illegible]	
	10		[illegible]	
	11		Depot was visited by the Corps Commander Lieut [illegible] A.D.O.S. V Corps.	

WAR DIARY
or
INTELLIGENCE SUMMARY.
(Erase heading not required.)

Army Form C. 2118.

D.A.D.O.S. 38th (Welsh) Div.
MARCH 1918

Place	Date	Hour	Summary of Events and Information	Remarks and references to Appendices
POULAINVILLE	MAR 12		Visited Division at A.O's.	
	13		Depot visited by A.D.O.S. V Corps.	
	14		Departure to Routine	
	15		O.O. 3rd Army Troops No2 arrived Poulainville from Corbie.	
	16		Visited Div. & H.Qrs.	
	17		Depot visited by D.D.O.S 3rd Army & A.D.O.S 3rd Army to form scheme for new Depôt and allocation of Ordnance reserves in vicinity.	
	18		War in progress for store accumulation for D.O.S	
	19		Routine	
	20		Inspection of Equipment of H.Qrs 13th Brigade & H.Qrs 22 Field Battery	
	21		Visited A.D.O.S V Corps H.Qrs. VIGNACOURT.	
	22		Amalgamations of O.O. 3rd Army Troops, OO V Corps Troops & D.A.D.O.S arranged, all forming one of prominent to be known as 9 C.S. POULAINVILLE. (See next Report)	
	23		Hangar for I.C.S (Receipt) completed.	
	24		Visited by A.D.O.S V Corps.	
	25		Stores to C.M.T. I.S. Depôt visited by Corps Commander Lt. Gen. Shute. surprised one being sent of valuable	
	26		Visited Division at H.Qrs	
	27		Conference at Fouq. P.R.E. to meet D.A.Q.G. 38th Div. & A.Q. MQ. 5th Corps to discuss the hurrying on of unit equipment.	

Army Form C. 2118.

WAR DIARY
or
INTELLIGENCE SUMMARY. D.A.D.O.S. 38th (Welsh) Div. MARCH 1919.

(Erase heading not required.)

Place	Date	Hour	Summary of Events and Information	Remarks and references to Appendices
POULAINVILLE	1919 MAR 28		Depot visited by A.D.O.S. VIth Corps.	
	29		Visited Divisional H.Q.	
	30		Routine.	
	31		Major Cox left for 14 day leave to England, handed over duties to Capt. F.W. Yell. F.R.A.O.C.	

Poulainville
3/0/19

[signature] Capt.
for D.A.D.O.S.
38th Division

WAR DIARY or INTELLIGENCE SUMMARY

(Erase heading not required.)

D.A.D.O.S. 38th Division.

Army Form C. 2118.

Place	Date	Hour	Summary of Events and Information	Remarks and references to Appendices
Bordeuville	1919 April 2		Visited Vecquemont sub-railhead.	
	3		Do. Divisional Newlaventure.	
	4		Depot visited by A.D.O.S. 5th Corps.	
	5		Visited Vecquemont - Conflie to ullivians men for transfer to R.A.O.C	
			Do. O.O. Army Troops No 4 in connection with stores and units transferred	
	6		22nd N. Divn. proceeded to England, G.1049 and to R.N.O.P 3rd Area	
	7		Inspected equipment of 13th, 14th, 15th & 19th Welch Regt. also 113th + 114th Brigade H.Q's and 14th R.W.F. at Cerisie Park	
	8		Gluy. Depot visited by Col Tufnell D.A.D.O.P. 3rd Area. Visited Commandant Cerisie Park Rangers and 10th S.W.B at Gluy, also O.C. Q.N.Q Autorage Vecquemont at Bleville.	
	9		Inspection of equipment of 13th Signal Section R.Q.A at Bleville	
	10		Visited Mericourt re new Railhead to open. Depot visited by General de Rougemont Commanding I Corps. Group Packet.	
	11		Inspection of 13th, 16th R.W.F's equipment at Gluiy, and 13th Field Ambulance at Longueau. Visited Divisional HQs.	

(1030) Wt W.3109/P713 750,000 3/18 E & 2688 Forms/C2118/10.
D., D. & L., London, E.C.

Instructions regarding War Diaries and Intelligence Summaries are contained in F. S. Regs., Part II. and the Staff Manual respectively. Title pages will be prepared in manuscript.

WAR DIARY or INTELLIGENCE SUMMARY.

(Erase heading not required.)

Army Form C. 2118.

B.A.D.S. 38th Division

Place	Date	Hour	Summary of Events and Information	Remarks and references to Appendices
Paturville	1919 April 12		Equipment inspection of "17th Rfl" (?) men at Clixy. Visited "win 2nd" H.Q. & Departmental portion.	
	13		Inspection of Equipment of 130th & 129th Field Ambulance at Clixy. Visited Divisional H.Qrs.	
	14		Inspection of Equipment of N.Ors. Visited subrailhead closed. Units to draw from Paturville. Ceremonial Sub-railhead closed. Units to draw from Paturville.	
	15		Depot visited by Brig. General Heade-Maker G.H.Q. and ODC	
	16		Turmell B.R.O.S. 3rd Area. Visited Infantry units at Clixy	
	17		Inspection of Equipment of :— Divisional Headquarters, Headquarters R.A. 121 Bde R.F.A.	
	18		Inspection of 122 Bde R.F.A. & Batteries, R.A.C. Inspection of R.E. 123rd Field Coy. R.E. Headquarters R.E. 123rd Field Coy, R.E.	
	19		Inspection of equipment of 124th Field Coy. R.E. 151st Field Coy. Do Do 115th Inf. Brigade H.Q.	
	20		Do Do	
	21		Visited 122 Bde R.F.A. re Demob. Stores Table.	

WAR DIARY or INTELLIGENCE SUMMARY.
Army Form C. 2118.

D.A.D.O.S.
38th Div.

Place	Date	Hour	Summary of Events and Information	Remarks and references to Appendices
Poulainville	1919 April 22		Visited Vecquemont Salvage Dump re Stores and Divisional Headquarters.	
	23		Visited 235 Div¹ Employment Coy at CORBIE re Stores Equipment inspection of Divisional Train.	
	24		Do Do Divisional Signal Coy.	
	25		Visited Headquarters R.E.	
	26		Apply visited by A.D.O.S. 3rd Army.	
	27		Visited 131 Field Ambulance re Dental Stores.	
	28		Do 5th Corps Q Packet Headquarters re visits to be made direct from there.	
	29		Visited Mericourt Railhead re visits to be made direct from there.	
	30		Arranged to take over certain stores from QMG Salvage Dump at Vecquemont.	

Poulainville
1/5/19.

[signature]
A.Q.M.G.
A.D.O.S.
38th Div.

[signature] Captain
A.D.O.S.
38th Div.